D0386325

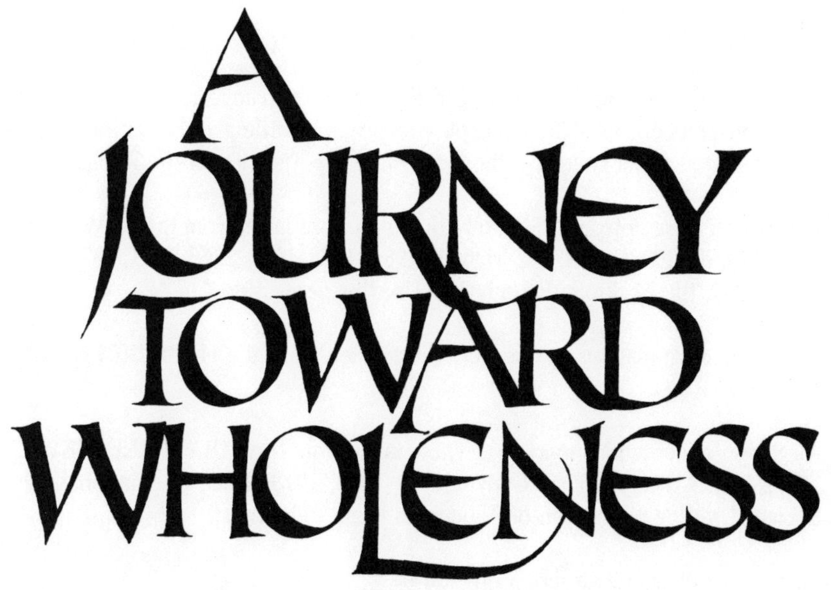


A Biblical Process of Healing, Restoration, and Joy

*Don Crossland*

NASHVILLE, TENNESSEE

Star Song Publishing Group, a division of
Jubilee Communications, Inc.
2325 Crestmoor
Nashville, Tennessee 37215

Printed in the United States of America
First Printing, October 1991

**Library of Congress Cataloging-in-Publication Data**

Crossland, Don.
A journey toward wholeness / by Don Crossland—1st ed.
p. cm.
ISBN 1-56233-022-5
1. Regeneration (Theology). 2. Crossland, Don. I. Title.
BT790.C75 1991
248.4—dc20 91-37404
CIP

2 3 4 5 6 7 8 9 10 — 98 97 96 95 94 93 92

# Dedication

o my wife Helen, who has exemplified God's unconditional love in an extraordinary way. Her passion for Christ and His righteousness has been like a brilliant beacon in the troubled sea, and her humor and wit has reminded me to take time to laugh and enjoy the rainbow, even in the darkest of storms.

*For I will not presume to speak of anything except what Christ has accomplished through me, resulting in . . . the power of signs and wonders, in the power of the Spirit . . .*

—Romans 15:18-19

# Acknowledgments

he writing of this book, as well as my own personal "journey toward wholeness," has included the blessing and encouragement of many along the way. It would be impossible to name every person who has had a part in my restoration or in helping to make this book a reality, but to all I feel a deep appreciation. I would, however, like to express my deepest thanks to the following people:

To Jane Stephens for typing the very first notes, consisting mostly of pain and hurt;

To Leah Springer and Karen Livingston who also spent many hours typing and correcting from notes and tapes;

To Stan Moser who read the original manuscript and believed the book would encourage others in their own journey or that of their fellow travelers;

To the group of Christian leaders who initially committed themselves to my restoration including James Robison, Rick Godwin, Peter Lord, Clark Whitten, Dudley Hall, Dick King, as well as my two pastors since my own resignation as a pastor, Jack Taylor and Jamie Buckingham;

To my board members, Joe Wylie and Bob Lilly, who continue to stand with me;

To Lisa Guest for her invaluable assistance in completing this manuscript;

To Matthew Price who has graciously guided the direction of the final manuscript;

To my mother and step-father, A. H. and Dorothy Lamm, who have faithfully supported me with their love and prayers;

Most of all, a special thank you to my wife and children, who so closely lived the pain involved as their husband and father began this journey toward wholeness.

# Contents

# Foreword

Reading through Don Crossland's manuscript I was reminded of a time back in the 70s when Don was a key player in the restoration of my own Spiritual journey.

I had developed deep anger and hurt and was broken to helplessness and discouragement about the Lord and His plan. It was Don who saw my pain and offered me a position on his staff even in the midst of his own struggles. His church, Highland Baptist, was like a soothing oil to my wounds as the Lord performed restoration in my heart. Like Don says in this excellent book, "restoration is an inner process that involves mending past hurts and finding healthy ways to deal with the unmet needs of the past. It is gaining insight into the past and determining how that past is affecting us today and then allowing God to turn our past hurts into present victory."

Through my pain and disappointment I truly found that Christ is sufficient for all my needs. I discovered Christ as my friend, healer, energizer and everything else I needed or ever will need. Don has not only discovered the same truth but he has thoroughly and effectively explained how you can turn sorrows into victory, your past pain into joy, and how Christ can actually transform an old beat-up discouraged person into the "Oak of righteousness."

My wife Norma and I have witnessed the transformation of Don and Helen's lives through the power of God's Spirit and His Word. This book pulls you to personally see that God's power is enough—that we can experience that transformation in our own lives.

May you discover the joy of God's transforming power as page by page Don explains it all so well.

—Gary Smalley
Phoenix, Arizona

# Introduction

If you're looking for a quick fix, you will be disappointed with this book. You won't find here three easy steps to wholeness or a secret formula for instant freedom from the unhealthy patterns of your life. What you will find, though, are the insights of one who has set out on his own journey toward wholeness and the personal application of those Scriptures which have guided my path.

## Accepting Lies As Truth

Many of us live according to false ideas about our worth as a person, ideas which often have their roots in painful childhood experiences. As we grew up, we accepted these lies as truth, and that perception of ourselves as flawed or inferior has affected how we've lived. We've undoubtedly developed ways of acting which protect us from being hurt or enable us to have our needs met by manipulating people around us. These systems of behavior seduce us into believing that we are living effectively. Our inaccurate and often unbiblical thinking about ourselves as well as those actions which stem from that thinking may seem quite right to us, despite our awareness of the fact that living outside of God's will leads to death.

## What Is Restoration?

Restoration involves more than stopping the patterns of behavior which harm us and other people. It involves more than adjusting the externals of our life. Restoration is an inner process that involves mending past hurts and finding healthy ways to deal with the unmet needs of the past. Restoration is not just behavior modification. It is the continuous action of change in the inner core of our being.

## The Process of Restoration

The process of dismantling our system of false thoughts and unhealthy actions and turning to God to meet our unmet needs and heal our past hurts is the process of restoration, and that process happens in three phases:

❖ First, you ***gain insight into your past***. A doctor needs to know your medical background so that he or she can treat you effectively. A correlation between problems in your past and your current health might help the doctor understand how to treat you. In the same way, it is important to understand the source of the lies and hurts you are dealing with in your emotional and spiritual life. I am not suggesting that you blame someone; I am suggesting that you learn at what point you can assume responsibility. Then you will be able to be released from the past, an important step toward restoration.

❖ Next, you ***determine how your history is affecting you today***. Delving into the past and staying there is not healthy. But the Holy Spirit, who convicts us of our sins, can give us insight about how our past is affecting the present. The Holy Spirit can show us how we are acting out the hurts or unfulfilled needs of the past. He can help us see and then release the lies we have accepted as reality. The Spirit can also help free us from the sinful systems of behavior that were our means of coping or surviving.

❖ Third, ***let God turn past hurts into present victory***. With new insight about ourselves and with the guidance of the Holy Spirit, we can let God work His gracious miracle and turn the hurts of the past into the victory of today. He does that for His people: "God causes all things to work together for good to those who love God" (Rom. 8:28) is a promise we can claim as we surrender our hurts, our failures, and our wills to our heavenly Father.

Looking carefully at our current thought patterns and behavior patterns will help us link them to our past hurts and unmet needs. When we make the link, then we can understand why we think and act the way we do, and we can begin the journey toward wholeness and the process which leads to healing, restoration, and joy.

## A Word of Encouragement

Let me encourage you to commit yourself to this journey toward wholeness. God has designed a path specifically for you, and He has people in His body who can come alongside you to help and encourage you. Find those people so that they can bear your burden with you, help you when you struggle, and rejoice with you when you experience the healing God has for you.

Let me also encourage those of you whom God has called to be instruments of His restoration and the redeeming power of Jesus Christ. Commit yourself to Jesus. Trust Him to give you the wisdom, the strength, the patience, and the love you need in this important ministry. Also, pray for the person you are helping who is in need of restoration. And may both of you witness anew God's grace as He walks before you and beside you on this journey toward wholeness, a journey of healing, restoration, and joy.

Don Crossland
Indialantic, Florida
October 1991

*Throughout the book, I share stories of people who have recognized their need for healing and restoration. I have changed their names to protect their privacy, and on occasion I have merged more than one person's story. May the experiences of these people remind you that you are not alone as you travel on your own journey toward wholeness.*

- *Why are you reading this book?*
- *Why do you want to learn about the restoration process?*
- *Be as specific as you can—there is no right or wrong answer!—and let those ideas guide you through the book and shape your prayers for your journey toward wholeness.*

CHAPTER ❦ ONE

# Breaking Denial

*My worst nightmare was unfolding around me: my world of secret sin was being exposed. The counselor with whom I had shared my struggles with sin had come to the door and asked if we could take a ride together. We drove through the quiet neighborhood where I lived. After a period of silence, he turned to me and said, "Don, I'm sorry. I let your sin of moral perversion slip in a conversation with one of the church leaders. It's all over." At that moment, it was as if a thousand knives pierced my heart.*

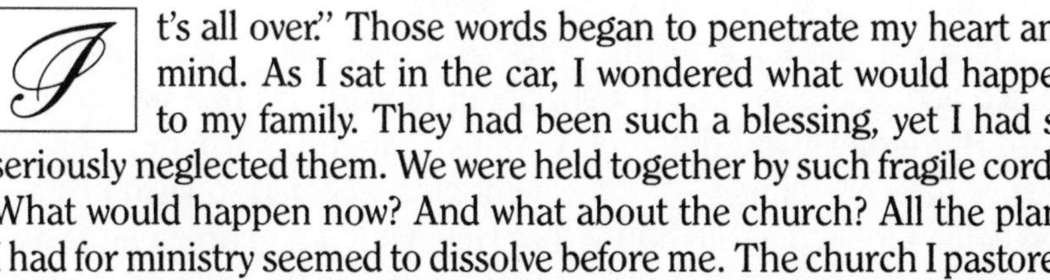

"It's all over." Those words began to penetrate my heart and mind. As I sat in the car, I wondered what would happen to my family. They had been such a blessing, yet I had so seriously neglected them. We were held together by such fragile cords. What would happen now? And what about the church? All the plans I had for ministry seemed to dissolve before me. The church I pastored and the ministry I had so graciously been given—these were gifts far beyond anything I had ever imagined for myself. We had just completed the architectural design for a 4,000-seat auditorium. We had purchased over fifty acres of land to relocate and to build upon. Every dream I had was just beginning to come true, but now—with the words, "It's all over"—those dreams began to vanish.

## "Whatever It Takes"

Just a week or two earlier I had gone out to the site of the new church building. Kneeling there that evening, I cried out to God in a very different and unusual prayer. Tired of the hypocrisy and the struggle inside, I prayed one of the most dangerous prayers of all. It went something like this: "Oh God, do whatever it takes to purify my heart." Though I meant it, I have to admit that I was terrified of the possible journey ahead. Perhaps the crumbling of the walls that had protected my secret world was the beginning of God answering that prayer.

The day after I first prayed that prayer, my wife Helen and I took a trip to Seoul, Korea, to participate in a conference on church growth. Again, I knelt before the Lord and prayed, "Oh God, do whatever it takes to purify my heart." I was tired of my secret world, my secret struggle.

I had been to a psychiatrist and various counselors, but they didn't seem to help. The futility of those sessions had pushed me to my knees, but never did I imagine how my prayer would be answered. As I prayed in Korea, I knew nothing of the events that would unfold over the next few weeks and how they would impact the years to follow. I had hoped that God would respond to my prayer in a more private way.

## Sharing My Secret

As the counselor continued to drive through the neighborhood, he asked me if I would like him to be with me when I shared the news with my wife. I said no. I felt betrayed and disappointed, but more numb than angry. I couldn't think clearly.

He drove me back to the house. I got out of the car and, as I walked across the yard, I thought about how often I had walked that path. But today it was different. On this beautiful, warm day—one of the last days of summer—the fresh-cut grass seemed so vivid in smell and color. I looked at the house that Helen and I had dreamed about, worked for, and finally purchased, and I realized that all of this could be lost when I resigned.

Helen saw me as I slowly walked toward the house, and she realized that something was wrong. I asked her if I could talk with her alone. We walked into the bedroom where we had sat so many times before to discuss various problems, and I began unfolding my story. As I spoke, I could see that she had a hundred questions, but she didn't ask them aloud. I could read in her drawn features, "Please tell me that this isn't real. Please tell me that this is a nightmare and that it isn't true." She didn't need to say those words; I knew what she was thinking and feeling.

As I completed my painful and tragic story, I told Helen that I would be meeting that afternoon with our church's leadership. I would then present my resignation. She sat in stunned silence for a moment longer. Then she slowly stood up and walked over to me. Although she was experiencing much anguish and pain, she simply said, "Don, I love you and I am going to stand with you."

Helen reached out to embrace me, and I felt the love of God flow through her in a way that was deep and wonderful. Suddenly I began to realize that the love which I had searched for in many different and wrong ways was plastic and artificial. I was now experiencing a touch of God's love through my own wife. I knew that this was only the beginning of finding what I had long been searching for.

## Talking to My Children

The next step was to talk to my children. I had to do that despite the numbness I felt inside. I asked my son if I could meet with him. As we sat in his bedroom, I saw from his face that he feared being reprimanded for something he had done. Slowly, I told him that what I had to share with him was the most difficult thing I would ever have to tell him. Then I told him about my moral perversion and explained that I would be resigning my position at the church. After a moment of stunned silence, he turned to me and, with tears in his eyes, said, "Dad, you and Mom have loved me all these years, and I am not going to stop loving you."

I reminded my son that this situation could be exposed in the newspapers because of the high profile of my ministry and the fact that our church was well-known in our city. I knew that my then-fifteen-year-old son might be embarrassed at school. He put his arms around me and said, "Dad, I love you and I want to stand with you." I asked him about the embarrassment that he might experience. He said, "If my friends reject me because of this, then they weren't really my friends."

Next, I had to talk to our daughter who was six months pregnant with our first grandchild. Again, I felt a horrible sense of shame as I shared with her the story of my sin. Though she showed no anger, I did see disappointment in her eyes. Once again, though, I heard words of love. She and her husband responded with, "Dad, we love you, and we're going to walk through this with you to recovery and restoration."

## Resigning from the Church

Besides bringing shame and disappointment to my family, I had also shamed the cause of Christ and the congregation He had entrusted to me. So when I met with the church leadership that afternoon, we planned for me to present my resignation to the congregation on Sunday evening.

As I stood before the people that night and slowly began confessing my sin and failure, I saw many different responses. Some wept, and others reacted with disbelief and surprise.

As I spoke, I wished that I had written out my confession instead of trying to share from memory. I found that my mind was going numb and I could hardly remember anything. Later I realized that, while some people thought I was being truthful, others thought I was being evasive. Only in retrospect did I realize how much better it would have been to have written out my confession with the help of counselors and spiritual leaders, people who knew and loved me and would not have been emotionally entangled in the situation.

Later, I did write out a confession that was read to the church. This written confession was somehow released to the local newspaper which in turn released it to the Associated Press. The entire situation would now be exposed in a way that I had never dreamed possible. I knew that I should prepare other family members for the information that would soon become public. I suffered through many difficult moments on the telephone, trying to explain to my relatives what had happened.

## Recognizing My Denial

As this chapter of horror unfolded, I felt so weak that I could hardly get out of bed. I didn't want to live. I wanted to escape, to be a little boy again (even though those days had their own unhappiness) and roam the orchards and cotton fields of my childhood.

Editors from several newspapers had already begun to call. One night at about 1:30 a.m., a reporter called under the pretense of an emergency, hoping that I would talk. I was having to face my secret world. I didn't want to admit it, but I realized even then that God was using these circumstances to bring me into reality and help me break denial.

It was at this time that a friend called and suggested that our family go out to his condominium on the Florida coast for a time to recoup. He offered us a shelter from the raging storm of publicity, and we accepted. As we headed to the Florida coast, I didn't have the strength to drive. Traveling through the countryside in the van, I felt as though I were in a coffin, rolling into oblivion. During the night, I lay in the backseat looking up at the stars and thinking. I knew I would either run from my problem or run to Jesus for His help.

I had prayed and sought out Christian counseling, but I was still held in bondage. I could not break free from my immoral ways. If this exposure was God's way of releasing me from my bondage to sin, then I would submit to Him. I resigned myself to the hand of God. I had many doubts, but I knew I could trust my heavenly Father. Besides, I had no other place to run and no one else to run to.

For the next two days of our drive to Florida, I sometimes wished that I had stayed on the farm where I was raised. Perhaps then my secret sin would not have been exposed to such a wide audience. But wishes like that would get me nowhere. I had to learn to face reality and to live in it. I could no longer live in the world of fantasy. I could no longer deny the part of my life I had worked so hard to hide.

Still I was haunted by the words, "It's all over." Was my ministry over? My marriage? What about my relationship with my children? How would my friends respond? And what would it mean for my future?

Somehow the Holy Spirit calmed my fears. He told me that "It's all over" meant far more than I could imagine and, in fact, it meant something much different than I thought. "It's all over" meant that I no longer needed to hide or be entangled by the guilt, shame, and self-hatred related to my secret sin. I could choose to continue living with the pain of deception, or I could begin the process of healing and restoration in a journey to wholeness. And I began that process of healing by recognizing the denial that I had lived with for so long—and that is the crucial first step for someone on the path of restoration.

## Refusing to Admit the Truth

What is denial? Webster's defines *denial* as the "refusal to admit the truth or reality," and that refusal can happen in many different ways.

❖ Some people say, "I don't have a problem." It's easy to deceive yourself like that. I know because, looking back, I see that I really believed I didn't have a problem. How could I have a problem, I had reasoned, as long as my sin was secret and no one was affected by it? Yet, as I looked back at the hours that I had wasted in my secret world, the finances that were involved, and the relationships with God and my family that had suffered, I knew I had negatively affected everyone around me and myself as well. "I don't have a problem" is a means of denial, a statement that denies the truth.

❖ A similar statement of denial is "What other people don't know won't hurt them." The truth is that our secret sin does hurt other people simply because secretiveness hurts relationships. When we are hiding something, we are unable to be transparent with another person. This lack of openness endangers the relationship and the trust that is key to its health. Our secretiveness can also make us more judgmental, especially when we are feeling guilty about our secret. When we look at people through our own guilt, we will often judge them unfairly. By looking at other people's failings—real or imagined—we can stay in denial about our own.

❖ Denial also manifests itself in the statement, "I can live in both the private, secret world of my addiction and the public world outside that addiction." People in denial convince themselves that, as long as their addiction is private and secret, they won't have to deal with any consequences of their behavior. While they may be able to avoid some consequences for awhile, they cannot avoid the spiritual consequences of their action. The sinful behavior to which they are addicted causes a block between them and the Lord. With this kind of defilement in our spirit, we are not clear instruments of God's love. In fact, we are not even being open and honest with God about where we need His help to repent.

❖ A person in denial may also believe, "I can handle this myself. I don't need anyone else's help. Besides, if someone knew about my problem, it would only hurt them." I told myself this many times as the church continued to grow and my ministry expanded. On approximately fifteen different occasions I wrote out a resignation, but then I convinced myself that, if I resigned, the church and my family would suffer. The truth is that an unconfessed secret sin does far more damage than a sin we confess. A sin we confess can be dealt with: we can be forgiven and we can change our ways. An unconfessed sin, however, is a festering sore that contaminates our relationships with others, our relationship with God, and our feelings about ourselves.

Probably the most serious symptom of denial is the refusal to admit the problem. When we don't admit we have a problem, we can't be helped. Our refusal to admit a problem may not be understood, however, by people who have never been in denial. Since my resignation, for instance, people have asked me how I could have preached and ministered when my life was a lie. I explained to them that I could minister because I had simply refused to admit that a problem existed. I had compartmentalized my secret world and separated it from every other aspect of my life. The Holy Spirit would remind me of my sinfulness, but on Sunday it was as though the problem didn't exist once I walked into the sanctuary. I lived in a fantasy world; I was living with the delusion that my secret was safe. I was denying the reality of my sinful ways.

The very first step toward wholeness is to break through our denial, our way of saying that we don't have a problem. Wholeness depends on the admission that there is a problem, and the movement toward wholeness begins with the recognition of one's spiritual bankruptcy and powerlessness, a recognition that enables us to embrace God's grace.

As we begin to break denial, we begin to face the consequences of our own actions. People who are involved in addictive and compulsive behavior and who are in denial about it do not have a sense of reality. They don't face the consequences, long-range or short-term, of their actions. When we break denial, though, we must face the consequences of our wrong actions—first in our relationship with God, then in our relationship with others, and finally as our actions affect us personally.

## Recognizing the Consequences

Several days after my resignation, I was reading the story of David's sin in 2 Samuel 11. When Nathan confronted David about his secret sin, Nathan asked the king why he despised the Word of the Lord by doing evil in His sight (2 Sam. 12:9). As I read those words, the Holy Spirit pierced my soul with that very same question. My first response was "God, I have not despised Your Word. I have loved and taught Your Word for years, memorizing and hiding it in my heart."

Then I came to Nathan's second statement—"You have despised Me" (2 Sam. 12:10). The Holy Spirit again spoke to me, this time telling me that I had despised God by not obeying Him. That evening I wept as I realized that I had sinned against God. My system of denial was being broken down further. I began to see the consequences of my wrong actions; I began to realize how God had viewed my sin and how it had affected my relationship with Him as well as with other people.

Whatever means God uses to break our denial, it may take us some time to fully realize the consequences of our actions. The situation is not unlike that of people who have been in a severe accident. They can't realize the full extent of the situation because of the pain they themselves are experiencing. Similarly, people in the process of breaking denial are often unaware of the pain they have caused other people because of their own acute pain. Yet, as they emerge from denial and their own personal pain begins to subside, they begin to recognize the pain that they have caused the people around them.

Breaking denial and accepting responsibility for our actions brings an awareness of pain, but these initial steps of restoration result in stronger and more open relationships with people close to us, especially our spouse. Many times, a husband or wife has long felt that something is not right, yet because they are ignorant of their mate's secret world, they questioned their own feelings and even their own sanity. It is important for the person breaking denial to face up to his or her responsibility to family members and to be open, honest, and genuine with them.

## Breaking Denial

Denial can be broken in a variety of ways, some of them more effective than others.

- ❖ Often—as in my case—denial is broken through exposure. It is important to point out that it is not exposure that heals or restores us, but that exposure may be a part of the healing process. Exposure can bring us into reality and force us to break our system of denial.
- ❖ Being confronted by a nonjudgmental, caring person can also help us break out of our denial and enable us to face the truth about ourselves.
- ❖ Confrontation from a judgmental and condemning person may worsen denial, though. The person being confronted may focus on the condemnation rather than the problem needing to be addressed. Also, people who are confronted in a hostile rather than a loving manner may easily find themselves justifying or rationalizing their actions, and this defensiveness can intensify their denial.
- ❖ Denial can sometimes be broken through unexpected blessings or success. The apostle Paul said that it is the kindness of God that leads to repentance (Rom. 2:4), but this path is the least probable way out of denial. Why? Because too often people misinterpret God's goodness to them as permission to continue in their sinful lifestyle.

However we come to recognize the problem we have been denying, we can break out of that denial by confession to someone who is in a position to help us deal with our problem. Often, though, we have too much pride or too great a fear of abandonment to confess our sin to someone. But when the pain of our secretiveness becomes greater than our concern for our pride or our fear of abandonment, we will be willing to talk to someone about our struggles—but we need to choose that person carefully. Confession to a person who can help is an important step on the road to recovery. Confession to someone who is not in a position to help solve the problem merely relieves our guilt. We feel better having told someone about our problem, but we stay stuck in denial rather than taking any steps toward changing those behaviors which cause our guilt.

When we make a confession to a person who can help, we find more than just the assistance we need. We find hope, and hope is a key ingredient to successful recovery. Even when there is a tremendous amount of pain involved, hope reminds us that God is there.

## Receiving a Promise

On the Sunday morning when we arrived at our friend's condominium, there seemed to be no hope, no future. I wanted the past to be a nightmare that would be gone when I awoke—but it wasn't. The past was a reality, and my attempts to deny it were failing. My system of denial was being broken; reality was becoming more real.

That morning, instead of standing before the congregations of hundreds that met at the church three times each Sunday morning, I found myself huddled together with just my family. This contrast was another painful step in my emergence from denial.

And how well I remember walking on the beach by myself later that day. I felt so ashamed of my actions, and I asked God if I was an example of His judgment. To my surprise, there was an answer so crisp, clear, and precise that I was stunned by its clarity. The answer came in this way: "You will be an example of My mercy, grace, and restoration."

How could this promise become a reality? At this particular point, I had no desire to minister again. I only wanted to slip into oblivion, to go somewhere and not be known. I wanted a simple existence of a hermit living in a cave.

Still, those words brought a hope that I began to cling to. That powerful promise would encourage me to walk with God in the days to come.

### *Your Own Story*

- *Think about a time when someone stood with you after you confessed a failing. What did he or she teach you about God's love for you?*
- *Review the various statements of denial listed under "Breaking Denial." Ask the Holy Spirit to show you if some aspect of your life needs to be brought into the light of God's healing love.*
- *Write a brief prayer, asking God to forgive you when you are blind to your own sinfulness and thanking Him for His gracious forgiveness and unconditional love.*

CHAPTER ❦ TWO

# Walking through the Wilderness

*As my family and I neared the end of our time in Florida, I thought about the reality I needed to confront. I was being forced to face head-on the problem I had so long denied, and, as a result, I was starting to understand my own powerlessness. I had been programmed to think that I was somehow in control of my own destiny, that I was the god of my life and the solution to my problems. I had to recognize my inability to live as God would have me live. Only then would I be able to receive the help and restoration which God alone gives. But little did I realize the full impact of facing this reality and just how important God's promises would be as I continued on my journey toward wholeness and entered a wilderness so bleak that no one dare face it alone.*

In Romans, Paul writes, "Now may the God of hope fill you with all joy and peace in believing, that you may abound in hope by the power of the Holy Spirit" (15:13). I had read this verse before, but the phrase "God of hope" had never meant to me what it did as my family and I drove home from Florida. As I clung to God during these dark days, I found in Paul's words hope for the future, hope for myself as well as for my family.

Needing desperately to hold on to something greater than myself, I also memorized a promise in Galatians: "For we through the Spirit, by faith, are waiting for the hope of righteousness" (5:5). Even though I was responsible for the denial in my life, I knew that behind my sin lay a system of addiction with areas of compulsive behavior that I would have to dismantle. This verse from Galatians promised me that, as I undertook this process, I could look ahead to that "hope of righteousness." At this point in time when I was breaking denial—when I was recognizing my powerlessness and lack of resources outside of God Himself—and entering a wilderness experience of pain and loneliness, I needed to claim this hope and the promise that God would restore me.

## Wounded Sheep

On the journey home from Florida, I thought about how I would deal with the very real consequences of my sin. It was one thing to walk on the beach, look at the vastness of the ocean, and recognize that God's power and His purpose were far greater than I had ever imagined. But now I had to face the practical realities of my sin, and the impact of what I had done seemed to increase with each mile we drove closer to home.

Along the way, Helen and I discussed how hard it would be to return to church, but we so wanted to be accepted by our church family. We felt such a need for the healing balm of God's people. We decided where we could sit in the sanctuary and be the least conspicuous. Though we knew it would be an embarrassing, painful, and awkward time, we needed the love, acceptance, and healing power of Jesus Christ that come through His people.

We arrived home early Saturday morning, and it wasn't long before two church leaders came to see us. We invited them in and, as they entered, I noticed the look of concern on their faces. When we began to talk, they shared with me that, since this should be a time of healing for the church, we shouldn't return to the church at all at this time. They explained that the congregation needed time to work through their anger and sense of having been betrayed; they needed time to heal. Furthermore, some members of the church doubted my repentance.

At first I didn't understand this attitude. I felt angry, and I was hurt. Now that some time has passed, I understand more clearly that wounded sheep cannot be healed by a wounded shepherd—or vice versa. The people I had pastored needed to experience the healing balm of Christ. Furthermore, I see now, this wounded flock would not have been able to help me heal.

## The Wilderness Experience

When the church leaders left our home that day, Helen and I held each other and wept. I felt so alone and isolated. Helen made a statement that, at the time, I resented. She said, "Don, I know it's wrong, but it's right." I had never really understood this favorite phrase of hers until that day. That afternoon, I realized that some things may seem unjust and wrong, but in reality God is preparing us for the things He has for us in the future. He uses apparently wrong circumstances to develop in us the inner qualities that we otherwise would not acquire.

In bed that night, I reviewed the conversation with the church leaders, especially the part about not being able to return to church as part of the fellowship. Although I wanted to be a part of that body of believers, the Holy Spirit reassured me that the leaders' decision was right. I knew that God had a different plan for my life and a new direction for me. I also recognized how the church had become an idol to me and how my ministry had become the basis of my identity and my self-worth. I began to understand the words God had spoken about Israel—"I will allure her, bring her into the wilderness, and speak kindly to her" (Hos. 2:14). My ministry had become my god, and now that god was being destroyed. God was using this wilderness experience, I realized, to remove me further from the source of my idolatry and to lure me unto Himself. There, like many believers before me, I could come to know Him better.

But I knew from the Bible that, even with God in control, a wilderness experience is never easy. It certainly wasn't for the nation of Israel. In *A Way through the Wilderness,* author Jamie Buckingham describes how the people of Israel complained to Moses about the bitter water they had to drink. Moses complained to God and God, in His mercy, made the water sweet (Ex. 15:23-25). Yet, as Jamie explains, God had planned for the people to drink the bitter water and to benefit from it. First, the calcium in the water provided a muscle relaxant that would ease their soreness as they trekked through the wilderness. Second, the magnesium in the water acted as a cleansing laxative that would protect the Israelites from their impure diet and provide health and wholeness for their wilderness journey. God knows what He's doing when He leads us through a wilderness experience. And God's way—the path which takes us to restoration—is not haphazard, unplanned, or determined by chance.

❖ As Scripture reveals, God often uses an enemy to judge the sins of His people. In the book of Habakkuk, for instance, the prophet asks God why Israel is being judged by Babylon, a nation far more wicked and sinful than Israel (1:3-17). God's purpose behind Israel's suffering at the hands of the Babylonians was to move Israel to where He wanted her to be. Even today, God will use world events, the circumstances of our life, and even enemies to move us—as He moved Israel—from where we are to where He wants us to be. Distressing situations are God's way of bringing us to the point where He can correct us.

❖ God also brings His people to repentance by allowing them to experience a period of probation or exile. God, for instance, did not send Moses into the wilderness to destroy him or his ministry. Instead, God's purpose was to strengthen Moses' character so that he could have a more fulfilling life and fruitful ministry. Today, thousands of years later, God still meets Christians in the wilderness to mold and strengthen their character.

As Jamie Buckingham points out, three types of people emerge during these wilderness experiences:

❖ Hermits simply want to retreat and live the rest of their days in seclusion. Isolating themselves in one-person caves, they never risk failure and never live up to their God-given potential.

❖ Nomads are never able to understand God's purpose or see what God is doing. In bitterness, isolation, and loneliness, nomads wander in the wilderness for the rest of their life, always trying to find hope and purpose totally apart from what God has planned for them and never experiencing the abundance that God offers.

❖ Pilgrims recognize that God brought them into the wilderness in order to perfect, purify, and complete that work of maturation and purification which God had begun in them. Pilgrims are only passing through the wilderness; they are headed someplace better. They have failed, they have received God's correction, and they are walking toward the promised land of milk and honey. If we are pilgrims, it is in the wilderness that we begin to understand the intimacy of the relationship we can share with God the Father, and we emerge from the exile to a period of restoration.

## "Abba, Father!"

While I was going through my wilderness, thoughts and emotions inside of me were like a volcano. I had an overwhelming desire to cry out in pain and anguish. I shared with Helen my need to get away, to go into the countryside and express out loud what I was feeling. I drove to a secluded lake nearby. There, as I knelt down in a fetal position, I sensed a deep wail rising up from within me. I cried out, "Daddy!" It was as though I was trying to repair something that had broken long ago; I was trying to figure out where I belonged. I wanted to return to my childhood home; I wanted an identity and a sense of my roots. But as I cried "Daddy," I heard the small voice of the Holy Spirit asking me to receive God's spirit of adoption.

I thought about Romans 8:15—"For you have not received a spirit of slavery leading to fear again, but you have received a spirit of adoption as sons by which we cry out, 'Abba! Father!'" (The Aramaic "Abba" means, literally, "daddy.") On that day, I realized that the One I was searching for and the One who would restore me was my heavenly Father, my heavenly Daddy. I began to know God in a way I never had before. In fact, for several months after this experience, I would wake up at two or three in the morning and sense the presence of God so fully that it seemed I could almost touch Him. On this trip to the lake, the love of the Father began to fill my soul.

## Sharing the Burden

Often in the wilderness, we are betrothed to God and there we learn that He is our source of hope, of purpose, of life. When we have been stripped of whatever idolatry had ensnared us and we experience the barrenness of the wilderness, we are in a position to seek God only. Then we can more clearly see that He is all we have and all we need, and we come to the point where we don't use other people to meet our needs. Instead, we begin to allow God to meet our needs in abundance, and it is from this overflow that we are then able to give to others.

But along this path of restoration—first with the stage of breaking denial and then with the wilderness experience—other people can seem very far away. We often feel abandoned and alone. In such times, hope comes from our personal relationship with God as well as from our relationships with spiritual leaders. In Galatians, we learn that those who are spiritual should help restore a fallen Christian brother or sister (6:1). Although we may think of people restoring themselves by simply stopping what they are doing on their own, Scripture clearly shows us that we can not bring restoration to ourselves. We need the help of spiritual leaders who come alongside us to bear our burden and minister correction, healing, and grace.

During my wilderness experience, God surrounded me with godly men and women who loved me and told me that they were going to help restore me. Some of these people called me; others took Helen and me into their homes for the weekend. Some friends had us join them for their church services. One minister in particular invited us out to dinner and treated us like very special people, not lepers. We deeply needed this love and support.

I also needed to have these caring people hold me accountable spiritually. A person like me who has followed the way of idolatry (I worshiped the church I wrongly thought I was building) will continue to seek out that idol for some sense of value and worth. It is therefore of great importance that we receive hope and encouragement from spiritual leaders who will pray with us and for us.

## Strength in the Lord

As we wander in our spiritual wilderness, we will find encouragement from spiritual friends, and we can find strength through prayer and meditation on God's Word. During my wilderness days, I meditated on the life of David. In 1 Samuel 30, I read that David and his people were living in a city named Ziklag. While the men were out on a three-day maneuver, Ziklag was raided by the Amalekites. The women and children were taken captive and the city burned. When David and his men returned and saw the devastation, they wept. They lifted their voices in anguish until they had no more strength. In their pain, the people spoke of stoning David. At this stressful time of crisis, the Bible says, the king "strengthened himself in the LORD his God" (1 Sam. 30:6).

How did David do this? What was his basis for hope? I believe that David's hope—like our hope must be—was fully anchored in God and that it came from his sense of what God's purposes really were. If we have a sense of God's purpose, hope will well up inside of us. As David sought the Lord's will, he gained a renewed sense of God's purpose and was able to rest in His plan for this particular situation. And so David found strength.

During our wilderness experience, we can strengthen ourselves in the Lord in several different ways. Like David, we can remember God's call to us and His blessings in our lives. David must have thought back to the time when God had chosen him and, through Samuel, anointed him to be king (1 Sam. 16). Day after day during my wilderness times, I thought back to the promise that God had given me on the beach, the promise that He would make me an example of His mercy and restoration.

I also remembered God's hand on my life when I was ten years old. I was hit by a car while riding my bicycle and dragged forty feet under the wheels of a trailer loaded with cotton. Most of the skin on my body was peeled off. I vaguely remember lying in the emergency room and hearing the doctor tell my parents that he wasn't sure I would live. Yet God in His mercy saved my life and miraculously healed my broken body.

I also took comfort in recalling how God had enabled me to attend college. Finances weren't available, but I was able to go to school on a basketball scholarship. I hadn't intended to try out for basketball, but I had been playing one afternoon when the basketball coach passed by. He watched me play and, that afternoon, offered me a full scholarship.

There were other instances of God's provision in my life, and those recollections of God's grace, power, and call on my life gave me the sense that my life still had purpose. My God was a God of hope, and I knew that He who had promised would surely fulfill His promise. I strengthened my faith in the Lord not by looking at the circumstances, but by focusing on the God behind the circumstances.

Like Peter walking on the water, we will always start to sink in despair and fear if we simply look at the storms (Matthew 14:29-31). But if we focus on the One who can calm the storm and who controls every aspect of life, then we are able to strengthen ourselves in the Lord, not weaken ourselves with fear about the circumstances. And a wilderness experience gives us plenty of opportunity to learn to focus on the Lord rather than the situation around us.

## A Matter of Perspective

The 1 Samuel passage I referred to above offers another lesson in experiencing God's strength. Before David prayed, he asked Abiathar the priest to "bring me hither the ephod" (1 Sam. 30:7 KJV). I noticed that, when David put on this priestly garment, he didn't simply pray about himself and his immediate concerns. Instead, his prayer was based on the kingdom of God; his prayer reflected a greater concern for God's kingdom than for his personal situation. It occurred to me that, unlike David's supplications, much of my prayer focused on me. I realized that if I continued with my self-centered prayers, I would miss what God wanted. So I began to pray as though I were putting on a spiritual ephod, and I asked God to teach me to pray as He wanted me to pray.

I thought about the Lord's Prayer and Jesus' instruction: "Pray, then, in this way: 'Our Father who art in heaven, hallowed be Thy name. Thy kingdom come. Thy will be done, on earth as it is in heaven'" (Matt. 6:9-10). A study of the Lord's Prayer shows that when we pray as God has taught, we are never praying a self-centered, merely personal prayer. People who pray the Lord's Prayer pray not for their personal advantage but for God's will upon the earth.

From then on, when I needed to strengthen myself in the Lord, I pictured myself putting on a priestly ephod. Then, as I prayed, I prayed for my family and my future in light of the kingdom of God.

I prayed for His will to be done and for Him to use my experiences from the past, my present situation, and my future in whatever way He pleased. What a peace came from these prayers! What encouragement and hope to know that I could have a part in God's kingdom plan!

## A Burning Bush

Praying for God's kingdom, I learned, meant not praying that my ministry be restored. Such a prayer, I realized, could be idolatrous. Instead, I needed to seek first the kingdom of God and His righteousness and rest in the promise that all other things would be given to me (Matt. 6:33).

I've come to believe that if we only seek restoration, we probably will not experience it. If we only seek healing, we will probably not find it. If we only seek deliverance, we probably will not discover it. But if we seek the Lord with all our heart, we will experience the healing, restoration, and deliverance that He has planned for us.

The Bible supports this thought. In 1 Peter, for example, we are told to gird our mind for action, to be sober in spirit, and to fix our hope completely on the grace which is to be brought to us at the revelation of Jesus Christ (1:13). We are not to fix our hope on a future ministry or a possible blessing, but on Jesus our Savior. As we fix our hope on Him, we find hope for the future.

Consider, too, the promise of Jeremiah 29:11—" 'For I know the plans that I have for you,' declares the LORD, 'plans for welfare and not for calamity to give you a future and a hope.' " All of us need the hope of this promise during our wilderness experience. We need to be reminded that God will work things out for the good of those who love Him (Rom. 8:28).

How well I remember those times on my wilderness journey when God gave me hope just as He gave Moses hope at the burning bush. Most of us in our lifetime will have some kind of burning bush experience. We will recognize some specific moment as God's way of telling us that the long wilderness experience is almost over.

My burning bush experience came almost two years into the process of restoration. One day, a well-known Christian author asked if he could interview me about my restoration experience for an article he was writing. After our telephone interview, I heard deep within my spirit the words, "This is the day star rising in your heart," a thought based on 2 Peter 1:19. The day star or morning star is the star which proclaims that the darkness is passing and the dawn is almost here.

The day star—available to all of us—marks the fulfillment of God's promise that the wilderness is passing, the darkness is over, and the dawn is about to break.

And how the truth of this Scripture has been exemplified in my life! With that phone interview, God seemed to say, "This is the day star rising in your heart." God had faithfully given me light through His Word and His Spirit during those first few dark months after my confession when I didn't know what the future held and I didn't know what to do. I had simply walked through each day, relying on the lamp of His Word and the promise He had given me—"You will be an example of My mercy and My restoration." Since the interview, though, the day star has risen in my life, the light of dawn is surrounding me, and I am beginning to see the hand of God in all that happened in the past.

## The Light of God's Hope

In the pitch black darkness of the wilderness, however, dawn can seem impossibly distant. There may be a suffocating depression rather than any glimmer of hope. Someone once defined depression as anger turned inward, and that underlying anger can mean self-destructive behaviors—including overeating or oversleeping. I know. I spent my first few months sleeping and eating a lot. I focused more on my circumstances than on God's ability to work things out for His glory. I believed the lies of the Enemy that I would never be able to do anything again and that no one would accept me. I even wrestled with thoughts of suicide.

God's light, though, appeared when people showed that they valued me simply by spending time with me. I was encouraged when someone would tell me how I'd been a blessing to them and to others. On several occasions people called to say that they loved and respected me even though they were grieved and disappointed by my failure.

During this time, I pictured in my mind the Lord holding precious jewels in His hands. Through that image, He seemed to be telling me that He was extracting from my life those things that were precious so that they would not be destroyed and that all that was not of Him was being consumed by fire. Our God is a consuming fire who saves us from our idolatry by removing it from their lives.

Hope. It comes through faithful and godly friends. It comes through the Bible and prayer. It comes to our soul through the message of the Spirit. And these gifts of hope enable us to continue through the wilderness in the process of achieving wholeness and restoration. As we undergo the painful surgery of God's love, we can cling to a hope in Him that will not disappoint.

## *Your Own Story*

- *When I needed to find strength in the Lord, I looked back on God's calling and special providence in my life. List here some of your touchstones of faith—those special blessings from God and specific circumstances when His hand in your life was especially evident. Return to this list the next time you find yourself in the wilderness.*
- *Praying the Lord's Prayer and extending our prayers to other people and to God's kingdom can give us peace during a wilderness time when we are easily overwhelmed by our own struggles and pain. List those people, situations, and concerns of the kingdom which—even if you're not in a wilderness right now—keep you from being self-centered in your prayers.*
- *What special verse of hope serves as your burning bush or morning star? Write it out here.*

# CHAPTER THREE

# Battling Sin

*The awful nightmare would occur at intervals. At times I was running from some kind of bigger-than-life terror. Other times I was immobilized by fear. Each time I woke in a cold sweat, always thankful that I had been dreaming. As awful as they were, I knew those dreams were important. Long-hidden memories were surfacing, helping me get in touch with the crippling events of my childhood that had been buried but reenacted in my addictive behavior.*

y time in the wilderness was a time of growing intimacy with Jesus Christ, and the Holy Spirit began to deal more deeply with me in the inner core of my being. My time in the wilderness was also a time of deep soul-searching. It was a time for me to face the very real consequences of my past mistakes and sins. In fact, during this time, I read over and over these words of the apostle Paul concerning restoration: "Brethren, even if a man is caught in any trespass, you who are spiritual, restore such a one in a spirit of gentleness; each one looking to yourself, lest you too be tempted. Bear one another's burdens, and thus fulfill the law of Christ" (Gal. 6:1-2).

As I looked carefully at this verse, I was especially intrigued by the word *caught*. In New Testament Greek, the word is *prolambano* which means "to be overtaken beforehand." Looking back at my life, I wondered if and when I might have been "overtaken beforehand." I wasn't looking to avoid responsibility for my actions. I alone was responsible for the choice I had made in the beginning, but I had reached the point where I felt beyond choice, where I felt powerless before my addiction. How could I have gotten to that point? What had contributed to my secret and sinful acts? Understanding that might help me dismantle the system and help me change the inner core of my being. Only with a change in the inner person can true restoration take place. So I began searching back over my own life for an indication of where I had been overtaken. When had the seeds of my addiction been planted?

## The Roots of Sin

As I looked back over the years, I began to realize that I was overtaken in childhood. It was then that seeds of addiction were planted.

I distinctly remembered, for instance, what I perceived as a cold and distant father. Taking care of the family's financial needs meant that he often worked away from home. When he was home, some of the lessons I learned from him planted seeds for my later system of addiction.

My childhood was characterized by a lack of emotional openness and human closeness. I was taught by example that men don't hug, men don't cry, and men don't show their feelings. On many occasions, I wanted to feel close to my father; I wanted to be hugged and held by him. The most vivid experience I can remember took place during a west Texas thunderstorm when I was a young child. Frightened, I ran into my parents' bedroom, crawled into bed on my father's side, and snuggled next to him. He immediately woke up and shoved me onto the hard floor. When my father asked me why I was crying, I told him that I was scared. He then reminded me that men don't cry. That memory alone showed me why I had become ashamed of my feelings and why I longed to be touched and held. It also showed me why addressing God as "Father" had always been awkward.

Another memory—once it surfaced—taught me even more about myself. At a clinic for sexual addictions and emotions, I remembered being molested when I was six and seven years old, first by a farm worker and then by a laborer who worked for my father. Although these memories had been buried for a number of years, they had always been taunting me. Something deep inside of me—something I could never explain—made me feel ashamed, hidden, and afraid to be open.

During my early teenage years, I witnessed sexual experimentation among other males. Although I didn't participate, I longed for the closeness they seemed to find with each other. I began to fantasize, and I started to believe the lie that male closeness involves some degree of sexual intimacy. It is important to point out that this belief system and the sin patterns it fostered began with a lie. Having believed one lie, we easily accept those that follow, and the lies soon seem to us to be truth. In time, we begin to live out the lies. Only sincere repentance and change within our inward person will free us from the grip of those lies.

## Overtaken by Sin Patterns

Over the past several years, as many people have shared with me their own experiences, I've been somewhat surprised by the great number of believers who have been overtaken by sin patterns even though deep inside they despised the activity they were involved in.

❖ A Christian in a small midwestern farming community, Bill was expelled from college for public obscenity. He was later arrested for public exhibitionism, and he lost his job as well as the possibility of obtaining a new one. As Bill shared with me his heartbreaking story, he explained how he had spent thousands of dollars and hours of time driving to faraway communities to live out his fantasy.

Bill desperately wanted to be free of his obsession, but he was not able to restore himself. Hoping to find out where his sexual activity had begun and where he had been overtaken, I asked Bill about his background. He remembered his father being very stern and aloof. In fact, his first memory was being spanked by his father in public. He was told not to play in a nearby irrigation waterway, but—as small boys do—Bill forgot that command and soon found himself soaking wet. His father, in a fit of rage, made him undress in front of a number of farmhands and then publicly spanked him. Bill vividly remembered the onlookers' sneers, the giggling, and the obscene remarks as he was being spanked. Later, Bill explained, he tried various kinds of sexual experimentation with neighborhood children. During puberty, he became involved in sexual play and experimentation with his older sister. In an incorrect way, Bill was dealing with the shame he had experienced as a child when he attached his need for intimacy, closeness, and acceptance to acts of exhibitionism. Sadly, those acts never eased the overwhelming sense of shame Bill felt.

❖ Jake was a Christian, although he had not attended church for a number of years when he came to see me. Raised by deeply religious parents, he was the second of two sons, and he remembered clearly the words his parents had often spoken. Never intending to hurt him, Jake's mother and father frequently commented that he was supposed to be their little girl. As a result, Jake was never sure of his own identity.

During his teenage years, Jake was deeply confused about his sexual identity. He became involved in pornography, and he began to engage in sexual fantasies. He found an identity for himself when he was accepted by a man whose masculinity he admired. In Jake's fantasies, this attachment became sexual, a learned behavior resulting from his involvement with pornography and his masturbation. When Jake later attempted suicide, counselors diagnosed him as a manic depressive, and he remained in a low-grade depression.

When a Christian man began to minister to Jake on a regular basis, however, a strong and healthy friendship developed. Jake eventually became involved in a church, and within two years he had experienced tremendous restoration in his life. He was enjoying a renewed relationship with his family and with God, and those relationships were a source of hope and healing. Later, Jake met and married a Christian woman and today they have a family. The process of restoration couldn't be rushed; there are no quick fixes. But, with prayer, perseverance, and God's blessing, Jake found freedom from an addiction that had its roots in his childhood.

❖ When Sue came to see me, I saw in her yet another person who had been overtaken. Sue was obese and unable to control her eating. She professed to be a Christian, was active in her church, and was greatly loved and appreciated by her fellow Christian believers, but her compulsion with food dictated her lifestyle.

Sue was raised in a large city on the West Coast by a father who was overpowering. He never allowed her to make personal decisions—even simple choices about clothing, hairstyle, friends, or activities. At an early age, when decisions had already been taken away from her, she hid candy and ate it whenever her father was not aware of it. By doing this, Sue gained a sense of control in her life. In reality, however, instead of being in control, Sue was controlled by her eating habits. Eating candy became an obsession. In fact, she would go to the store, head to the candy section, and fill her cart. She would then take all that candy home and lock it in a cabinet. When her family was gone, Sue went to the cabinet and lived out her fantasy of being in control. The huge amounts of candy she ate gave her a sort of high—and resulted in her obesity.

After Sue began to understand that the issue of control lay behind her eating, she began to deal with the pain of the past. She also joined the chapter of Overeaters Anonymous which her church sponsored. With this ongoing support, Sue has experienced a degree of success. She still struggles, but healing and restoration are becoming realities in her life.

The stories of Bill, Jake, and Sue may seem extreme, but sadly the list could go on and on. Food, drugs, alcohol, sex, work, gossip, rage—people in the body of Christ fight addictions to these and other things. An expert on addictions shared with me that as many as twenty to thirty-five percent of the ministers in all denominations exhibit an addictive behavior in their life. Ministers or laity, believers have often been overtaken by some thought pattern or defense system that is now controlling them.

## The Struggle with Sin

Where do these controlling systems come from? As I've said, they seem to have their roots in childhood experiences. Because of experiences in their past, people can feel ashamed of their legitimate needs for intimacy, love, and care; for security, safety, protection, and purpose; and for having opinions, setting goals, and maintaining a clear sense of self. The basic needs which Bill, Jake, Sue, and I had—the need for closeness, acceptance, control—were not met in appropriate ways when we were younger. Consequently, Bill, Jake, Sue, and I searched (sometimes consciously and sometimes unconsciously) until those needs were met, and our needs were met in inappropriate, unhealthy, and even sinful ways.

Once needs are being met, it is often hard to escape from the system we've developed, even when, like Bill, we desperately want to escape our behavior patterns. Professing Christians who don't understand the power behind their actions often want to be freed and restored, but the battle rages. In Romans, Paul writes about this struggle: "For we know that the Law is spiritual; but I am of flesh, sold into bondage to sin. For that which I am doing, I do not understand; for I am not practicing what I would like to do, but I am doing the very thing I hate" (7:14-15). For Bill, Jake, Sue, and me, our actions were a mystery which seemed to have no logic. This is not to say that we were not responsible for our actions. Even in an addictive lifestyle, the addicted person is responsible for his or her actions and choices. But there may come a time when our actions seemed out of our control. Such is the case of those who have been overtaken.

A person addicted to an unhealthy way of meeting basic human needs may not be sinning by intent. Instead, that addiction is a stronghold which makes people do the very thing that, in their spirit, they do not want to do. It is important for believers who are overtaken to understand what the apostle Paul understood: "No longer am I the one doing it, but sin which indwells me. For I know that nothing good dwells in me, that is, in my flesh; for the wishing is present in me, but the doing of the good is not" (Rom. 7:17-18). The sin pattern—our addiction—overwhelms the good we want to do. And that sin pattern is not who we are in Jesus; that pattern is not part of our true identity in Christ.

In Romans 7:14-20, Paul writes honestly about the human struggle to do the good we want to do, and he acknowledges that he is not able to do the good that he wants to do because of his fleshly habits. Every person who has struggled to escape a system of addiction knows the frustration of wanting to change and being unable to.

Then, in verses 21-25, Paul offers words of hope: "Wretched man that I am! Who will set me free from the body of this death? Thanks be to God through Jesus Christ our Lord! So then, on the one hand I myself with my mind am serving the law of God, but on the other, with my flesh the law of sin" (24-25). Paul recognizes his need to be freed from his old and sinful behavior which makes him feel so wretched. People who have been overtaken by unmet needs and ensnared by systems of addiction will finally reach the point of crying out, like Paul, "Wretched person that I am. Who will save me?" In my case, I simply cried out, "Somebody please help me!"

## The Power of the Gospel

What kind of help do people trapped by systems of addiction need? Sometimes, the person doesn't need restoration as much as regeneration, that gracious gift of new birth in Jesus Christ whereby we are made a new creation. Many people profess the name of Jesus Christ without possessing the life of Jesus Christ. These persons are like clouds without water. Void of the Spirit of God, they nevertheless join with believers and even become church leaders without ever experiencing the regenerating power of Jesus Christ. These people who don't have the Spirit of God within may not be free from whatever has overtaken them simply because they have never been born-again.

A great number of Spirit-filled people—people who have been born anew in Christ—have also been overtaken and need to be experience restoration. And God's grace has been made available to us through the gospel of Jesus Christ. As Paul says, the gospel "is the power of God for salvation to everyone who believes . . . For in it the righteousness of God is revealed from faith to faith; as it is written, 'But the righteous man shall live by faith'" (Rom. 1:16-17). We first experience the power of the gospel through faith when we trust in Christ for our salvation. We experience that same power as we trust in God to help us live out the Christian life day by day.

Many of us, however, have walked in our salvation as though it were a one-time experience, an event that has no continuing application or effect in our life, but the Bible teaches otherwise. Christ died for our sins, but He is also our life in the present. As Paul says, "The life which I now live in the flesh I live by faith in the Son of God, who loved me, and delivered Himself up for me" (Gal. 2:20). As we receive Him as Lord of our life, we are receiving His power and His forgiveness for our sins. Many people have received forgiveness for their sins, but they are not experiencing the full provision of the gospel whereby the life of Christ can be lived through them. We are to stand in the faith of Jesus Christ and the power of the gospel. If we aren't constantly living the gospel and walking in faith, then we will walk in the flesh and never experience restoration.

Understanding what restoration is means, in part, understanding the difference between the spirit and the soul, something I'll discuss more fully in Chapter 11. During the process of restoration, our soul—our mind, will, and emotions—may still respond to old patterns of thinking and acting. Even though we may have experienced regeneration and new birth in our spirit, our mind, will, and emotions will still contain the data, feelings, and thoughts of the past. Scripture calls this the "body of this death" (Rom. 7:24) that needs to be "done away with" (Rom. 6:6) and put off (Eph. 4:21-32). Unless we experience a transformation of the mind as well as new birth in our spirit, we can continue to walk in areas of bondage. We will still be overtaken; we will still need to be freed.

This old system—this body of death—is not easy to shed. The old consists of those activities that we dislike yet do anyway (Rom. 7:19); the lifestyle patterns which we set before salvation (Rom. 7:20-21); our bondage to old sin patterns (Rom. 7:23); and a sense of hopelessness as we wish to serve God but fail on our own power (Rom. 7:25). Identifying this fleshly system of behavior and thought and acknowledging its power will enable us to begin the process of dismantling our system of addiction. This process must also involve living in harmony with the life of Jesus Christ and living out His power within us.

## Spiritual Warfare

The process of restoration—the process of shedding our body of death and escaping from patterns of bondage—will mean spiritual warfare. And God provides His armor to help us succeed (Eph. 6:10-12). Paul tells us to gird our loins with truth, don the breastplate of righteousness, walk in the gospel of peace, take up the shield of faith, put on the helmet of salvation, and have with us the sword of the Spirit (Eph. 6:13-17). Only then will we be prepared to successfully "stand firm against the schemes of the devil" (Eph. 6:11).

Can you imagine going into battle without equipment to protect and defend yourself? Many people today do just that because they have no understanding of spiritual warfare. Neither did I. I had read the Scripture which said, "Be of sober spirit, be on the alert. Your adversary, the devil, prowls about like a roaring lion, seeking someone to devour" (1 Pet. 5:8), but I had never focused on the word *devour.*

Looking back over my life, I could see the schemes the Enemy used to devour and destroy, but at first I was reluctant to share with anyone the demonization that had played a part in my being overtaken. I believed that other people would think that I was avoiding responsibility with the old phrase, "The devil made me do it." I had to take responsibility for my sin and face the very real consequences of my actions, but that didn't mean I couldn't acknowledge Satan's role. The Enemy had overwhelmed me and brought defeat to my life, as I am sure he is now attempting to do in the lives of many. We can stand strong against this prowler, though, if we understand spiritual warfare and put on the armor God provides.

Key to the armor of God is the Word of God (Eph. 6:17). Our protection against the powers of darkness must include God's Word because its truth exposes lies (Matt. 4:1-11); the gospel of Jesus Christ because it is the power of God for our salvation (Rom. 1:16); and "the blood of the Lamb" and the word of our testimony because our own story of faith reminds us of God's call on our life (Rev. 12:10-11). Jesus Himself relied on the powerful truth of God's Word when Satan confronted Him in the wilderness (Matt. 4). Can we His followers do less and expect to be prepared for a confrontation with the Enemy?

We can also find strength and assistance in the battle in a community of Christian fellowship. The power of prayer and the encouragement we receive from our brothers and sisters can keep us walking through the wilderness experience and offer us protection from the Enemy. Receiving the teaching of a pastor, worshiping God regularly, and being held accountable in a community of believers can help us stand strong when Satan attacks.

One reason why so many people find themselves walking a path of recovery and restoration today is that they failed to get involved in a community of Christian fellowship for encouragement and spiritual governing. Such encouragement and accountability are crucial to all believers, including—perhaps especially—believers who are being restored. These believers need the extended Christian family to support them in the healing and maturing process (Gal. 6:1-2; Heb. 10:23-25 and 12:12). A person being restored often comes from an inadequate family system and therefore needs healing, loving support, and spiritual role models (1 Tim. 5:1-2). Accountability is also necessary for restoration because secretiveness, deception, and dishonesty have been a way of life. A spiritual leader who truly loves us and cares for our spiritual welfare will prove invaluable to our restoration (Heb. 13:17).

Restoration is not an easy process, but it is not an option for believers (Gal. 6:1-2). Some of us need to commit ourselves to the process of restoration God has designed for us. Others of us need to be willing to be used in people's lives as instruments of the healing power of our Redeemer God. Whether at this point we are being restored or are coming alongside someone in the process of restoration, we can trust that Jesus is with us, enabling the healing and teaching us more about His wondrous love.

## Your Own Story

- *Where do you still feel in bondage to your sinful nature? Do you struggle to control your tongue? Is your critical nature hard to lay aside? Do you sometimes do things that don't glorify God? Be as specific as you can as you confess to God where you are struggling against your old sin nature.*
- *Whether or not we are struggling to dismantle a system of addiction, each of us needs to rely on the armor of God. What element of the armor can help you in the struggle against sin you just confessed? Also, how do you rely on the power of God in your day-to-day living?*
- *Write a note of thanks to someone who came alongside you when you were struggling in a spiritual battle against the Enemy. Or, if you know of someone who is struggling right now, send him or her a note of encouragement.*

CHAPTER ❦ FOUR

# Hearing God's Truth

*In my mind, real men drank, swore, fought, and bragged about their sexual conquests. Also in my mind were my father's words—"You're not much of a damned man and never will be." Since my personality didn't seem to fit the mold I had long held up as the standard, I concluded that my dad's words must be true. He had spoken these words during my teenage years after I had made the commitment to enter the Christian ministry, and his words had ensnared and haunted me.*

Breaking denial, walking through a wilderness of pain, and battling our old sin nature—we could do none of this without God's grace, but not everyone reaches out and receives God's grace. In fact, the writer of Hebrews tells the church to "see to it that no one misses the grace of God" (Heb. 12:15 NIV), implying that some people would do just that.

Scripture teaches that God will supply the grace we need whatever the circumstances of life (2 Cor. 12:9). Even though we may have been the victim of unfair events and the Enemy has sought to destroy us, we are still responsible for responding to the grace of God. Even in a wilderness of pain, we can experience God's abundant grace. We can open ourselves to receive His forgiveness, His love, and His healing touch. We can open ourselves to hear and act on His truth.

## God's Threefold Truth

The creation story in Genesis teaches that human beings are made in God's image, in His likeness, and in order to share His dominion (1:26-28). This truth holds the key to freeing ourselves from our godless systems of addiction. Let's look closely at this threefold truth.

### *God's Image*

"Let Us make man in Our image," God says in Genesis 1:26, and God's image is His *being,* His eternal glory, and His perfect character. The apostle Paul writes, "But we all, with unveiled face beholding as in a mirror the glory of the Lord, are being transformed into the same image from glory to glory" (2 Cor. 3:18). When we deny this truth about ourselves, we reject God's intended purpose for us—we don't glorify Him—and we don't live out the righteousness characteristic of His image.

### *God's Likeness*

God continues: "Let Us make man . . . according to Our likeness" (Gen. 1:26). God is a God of order, and this truth is evident in the created world. In all of creation, we see God's order; He is not the author of confusion (1 Cor. 14:33). God's order is reflected, for instance, in His creation of male and female in the plant and animal worlds, the husband-wife relationship of human beings, the progression of the seasons, the movement of the planets, and the body of His church (1 Cor. 12).

When we acknowledge the order of the sexes, for instance, and act in accordance with that God-given order, we will experience a sense of *belonging*. A sense of God's order in the world helps us know both where we belong and that we belong. When we step out of the order God has ordained, we rebel against God's perfect design for us.

Notice, too, the word "us" in God's pronouncement. "Us" is a plural form that suggests God is speaking to another person or persons. God is, therefore, a God of relationship. Being created in God's likeness, then, involves us being in relationship with others, and those relationships are to rightly reflect the male-female order of God's design.

### *God's Dominion*

Finally, God says, "And let them rule over the fish of the sea and over the birds of the sky and over the cattle and over all the earth, and over every creeping thing that creeps on the earth" (Gen. 1:26). By entrusting us with the earth He created and placing us stewards over the planet, God gives each of us significance and a *purpose* for life. Apart from God, this need for significance can become self-seeking and destructive.

## Human Development: A Reflection of God's Truth

God has created us in His image, in His likeness, and to share His dominion and, interestingly, His design for our emotional and social development reflects this fundamental threefold truth. Note how the patterns of childhood development parallel the needs God created in us and the serious consequences when those basic human needs are not met (see the chart at the end of this chapter for a summary).

## GOD'S IMAGE/Our Sense of Self

From birth to age three, children begin the lifelong process of developing a sense of self, a sense of being. If a sense of identity is not developed early on, they will spend a lifetime trying to figure out who they are.

During this period, children are totally dependent on parents or caregivers for the touching, holding, feeding, hugging, and caressing which provide a sense of self. Discipline, the setting of boundaries, and the facial expressions of those people caring for them will also give children a sense of who they are. At this time, children also need the freedom to explore and to do. Their job is to act on their natural curiosity and discover their world.

### *Unmet Needs and Their Consequences*

❖ When children's basic needs are not met, their future growth is sabotaged. As they grow older, they will try to fill the vacuum left by unmet needs, and those efforts may not always be healthy. Also, these children may develop a private self, a sense of shame about those needs which weren't met, and a sense that they are unlovable. (Let me add that such sabotage is not always intentional. Sometimes it is and sometimes it isn't. Satan, the murderer and destroyer, is always trying to work through people to sabotage. He not only works through individual people but also through family systems and generations.)

❖ Lack of care at this time sabotages the children's future by teaching them that they don't matter. When they feel that they don't matter or experience abandonment or rejection—real or perceived—they learn from their feelings that they are unimportant.

❖ One young man's parents often told him, "When you were born, we really couldn't afford you." I realized that until Jim dealt with that statement, he would be living out the consequences of believing that lie. He needed to recognize that the statement was false: his parents had unintentionally conveyed that they couldn't afford him and that material possessions were more important to them than he was. In actuality, their comment was simply an observation that they were going through a difficult financial time when he was born. Playing the statement over and over in his mind, though, Jim had come to believe that it was true. In fact, he so believed it that he subconsciously lived it out as an adult by being constantly on the edge of poverty himself. Insight into the falseness of that statement helped Jim let go of the lie and start living according to the truth.

❖ Sometimes parents who wish their child were a different sex teach that child to be ashamed of his or her sexuality.

❖ Parents' unrealistic expectations make children feel that they must hurry and grow up. These expectations rob children of their childhood. The children end up living out roles and systems that were never intended for them.

❖ Slapping, overcorrection, or a continuous scowl can also sabotage a child's sense of self.

❖ Unmet early childhood needs will hinder and perhaps even arrest a child's emotional and psychological development. A person may spend a lifetime trying either to meet these needs or to ease the pain of having had them gone unmet, and their efforts too often lead to addiction, drugs, alcohol, obesity, and inappropriate sexual activity.

❖ If a child does not develop a sense of being, that child may develop a sense that he or she is flawed (a sense of *not* well-being) or, even worse, a sense of non-being. Most of us at some time have met people who do not have a sense of who they are. Like chameleons, they become like the people they admire. In quest of an identity, they begin to look, dress, and act like someone else. They become people-dependent and people-addicted, having no sense of self and always striving to be like another person. Striving to be like a role model can be commendable, but that striving should not be at the expense of our own uniqueness and sense of being.

❖ If children aren't affirmed during the first three years of their life, they may become performance-oriented, trying to gain the approval of people around them by doing what those people want or what the children think they want. The children's fear of losing whatever approval they do sense, however, may result in a lack of creativity and a fear of initiative.

❖ Children who do not develop a sense of being may never develop a sense of well-being. They will go through life feeling that there is something basically flawed and deeply wrong with them. Even as Christians, they may remain in this state until restoration takes place.

## GOD'S LIKENESS/Sense of Order and Sexual Identity

From the ages of three to seven, children develop a sense of order and belonging. One basic aspect of this sense of order is the recognition of gender difference. During these years, children begin to understand the difference between maleness and femaleness. Also during this period, they begin to understand the world of the family, of mother and father, of siblings, and of school. They learn basic lessons about power, boundaries, social relationships, and friendship. Small children's talk about whom they are going to marry indicates that they are developing a sense of sexuality, an identity, an understanding of relationships, and a knowledge of who they are in relation to other people.

*Unmet Needs and Their Consequences*

❖ When there is a lack of bonding with either parent, a child's gender identity can be sabotaged. Our relationship with the same-sex parent helps us begin to gain a sense of our maleness or femaleness; we begin to gain a sense of acceptance by the opposite sex through our relationship with our opposite-sex parent. Sexual, emotional, or physical abuse can result in a distortion of gender identity and a deep shame which can render a person emotionally crippled and socially isolated.

❖ The need for nurturing and acceptance can lead to sexual curiosity and experimentation. Later in life, still in quest of the mothering and/or fathering they never received, these children may turn to inappropriate sexual contact.

❖ Lack of bonding with parents can also result in the children's distrust of authority.

❖ Children who never developed a clear sense of their sexual identity because of childhood sexual abuse may also lack boundaries and a sense of personal authority. The early violation of their body—their physical boundaries—makes it difficult, except by the grace of God, for them to set boundaries for themselves when they are older. The inability to say no to a request and the feeling that life is out of control are two other serious consequences of sexual abuse.

## GOD'S DOMINION/Sense of Purpose and Dominion

From the ages of seven to twelve, children develop a sense of purpose as logical thinking develops and they learn how to learn, acquire basic skills, and identify inherent abilities. At this point, children more fully experience the reality that God created human beings to have dominion because children are feeling more capable and confident about functioning in the world.

*Unmet Needs and Their Consequences*

❖ These needs to develop skills and to learn to think logically can be terribly sabotaged when no one is available to teach children to learn and to help them gain the confidence that comes with recognizing one's abilities. This lack of modeling and mentoring is a very destructive form of abandonment.

❖ Children who are abandoned in this way easily develop an inferiority complex. They may become very passive and unable to set boundaries to protect themselves, or they may become aggressive, protecting their boundaries at any cost or crossing other people's boundaries in quest of dominion.

## Receiving the Truth

Perhaps, as you were reading about the three stages of development, you recognized yourself in some of the descriptions of unmet needs and their consequences. If you did, you probably sense that these needs unmet in childhood are insatiable. In fact, they never can be met by anyone except our heavenly Father. Our infinite and omnipresent God can touch our hurts from the past and meet those needs which have long been unmet.

When we do cry out to God, "Daddy! Father!," we can begin our journey to fullness and completeness. This will mean grieving our loss and then saying good-bye to the past while we let God our Father reparent us. This means traveling the road to restoration and, along the way, caring for the little child within, and the following exercises may help:

## Unmet Needs for Being

❖ Focus on God's love and acceptance. Do a Bible study on God's love, and ask Him to help you hear those verses as if He were speaking directly to you. Inserting your name can help personalize the verses for you.

❖ Ask God what He thinks of you. You'll be astounded by what you hear in your spirit. Allow God to fill in the gaps in your soul that never got filled. This time of accepting God's love will enable you to extend it to others.

❖ Spend time with the child inside of you. Read something light, eat at your favorite restaurant, sightsee, go for a walk, do whatever is just plain fun for you.

❖ Enjoy the fellowship of other believers. Let them mirror God's love and acceptance for you. Remember, they can't meet all your needs, but they can definitely be God's love with flesh and bones!

## Unmet Needs for Identity and Belonging

❖ Spend some time thinking about Jesus' words, "I am the way, and the truth, and the life" (John 14:6).

—As the way, Jesus is directive. To be directive is to be the initiator; to be forceful and willing to confront when appropriate.

—As the truth, Jesus is objective. To be objective is to be logical and analytical, to use one's reason.

—As life, Jesus is subjective. To be subjective is to be sensitive, perceptive, intuitive, and creative.

These three elements complement one other, and one without the others means a life out of balance. Where are you out of balance? Set a specific goal for one area where you want to be stronger and develop a plan for reaching that goal.

❖ We free ourselves from unhealthy dependent relationships when we develop relationships with a variety of people and build a broad support group for ourselves. We may need to learn to give or we may need to learn to receive. Choose someone you want to get to know better and set a goal for this week. How will you work on nurturing that relationship?

❖ The body of Christ is the greatest instrument for healing available in the world. There we have the opportunity to experience an extended family. We need to be cautious about setting expectations that are too high or too heavy for one person, but we can turn to God's people to experience some of what was missing as we were growing up. What church activity will you get involved in over the next month or so? Be specific.

## Unmet Needs for Purpose

❖ Write out some goals for yourself. What do you want to be doing in five years? In ten? What dream vacation are you saving for? What educational goal(s) would you like to reach in the next several years?

❖ Learn how to negotiate assertively but not aggressively. Does the community college in your area offer a class in communication? Do you have a friend whom you can learn from by listening to his or her way of asking for a favor or saying no to a request?

❖ Learn a new skill. Choose an activity that is important to you and your sense of self-worth. Again, consult the community college catalogue or the offerings of the local Y. Perhaps a friend could teach you basic auto mechanics, how to bake bread, or what to do with a needle and thread.

❖ Begin to discover your spiritual gifts and identify God's specific purpose for your life. Each of us has a special ministry in His kingdom, but not all of us know what that is. The body of Christ can help us identify our gifts and often can provide an opportunity for us to use those gifts to serve God and His people.

## When the Truth Is Hidden

Perhaps in the past, these truths about God and about who you were created to be were distorted, muffled, or ignored. That was Brent's situation, and his life clearly illustrates what happens when we ignore or suppress God's truth and its implications for how we are to live.

While attending seminary in preparation for the ministry, Brent was painting houses on the side. Because he did good work, his business grew, and he had to hire some additional people, including a secretary to help him with the bookkeeping. Brent, a Christian who said he wanted God's best for his life, began dating his secretary. Over a period of time, he became involved with her sexually.

I remember the day Brent came to see me. With tears in his eyes, he told me he had a strong desire to break free of his bondage. He confessed that he had acted immorally when he stayed with his girlfriend over the weekend. I asked Brent what his true motive had been when he hired his secretary. He sheepishly admitted to me that, although she was not as capable as other applicants, he had been sexually attracted to her.

As he allowed the Holy Spirit to reveal his motives, I asked him if the secretary was a Christian, and he admitted that she wasn't. He did say that, when he hired her, he'd hoped he would have an opportunity to witness to her. Did he want to marry her? Had he shared the possibility of marriage with her? He admitted that he had, even though deep inside he knew that she was not the girl God wanted for his life. Still, Brent had continued on in the relationship, denying that he was living outside of God's will.

I finally asked Brent if he would acknowledge that when he had violated his conscience, he had repressed the truth of what God wanted for his life. At first Brent didn't know exactly what I was talking about, but he had some sense that he had gone against the truth of Scripture. His moral violations had been a violation of God's character and image, an image we are created to reflect. Brent's sexual involvement with his secretary was not bringing God glory, and it was perverting the identity of the woman and what God wanted for her.

Whenever we suppress God's truth the way Brent had suppressed it, we will experience the "tribulation and distress" due every person "who does evil" (Rom. 2:9). There was great tribulation and distress in Brent's soul just as there had been in mine when I strayed from God's path of righteousness. If Brent could admit that he hired the secretary because of his sexual attraction to her, then the lie he was living would be exposed and he would take a step toward freeing himself from his distressing ways.

## Lessons to Learn

After sharing with Brent the truth that he was made in God's image, in His likeness, and to share in His dominion, I saw tears in his eyes. Brent confessed that he had ignored God's desire for his life. He had blocked the presence of God's glory and character in his own life, and he had interfered with God's desire for the woman he had violated. Brent realized that before he could completely dismantle sin in his life, he had to sincerely repent for exchanging the truth of God for a lie. And Brent did repent of his sin and turn to God for guidance in His way.

Fortunately, Brent learned a lot from his experience—and so can we.

❖ When our emotional and psychological development is arrested by unmet childhood needs, we may spend a lifetime trying to have those needs met. Unless we receive the grace of God and find wholeness in Jesus Christ, we may try to meet our needs in illegitimate ways and so add a burden of shame on top of our childhood pain.

❖ We should not be ashamed of unmet needs. Instead, we should embrace our weaknesses (not our sins) and let the strength of Christ be perfected in us. When we acknowledge the childhood needs which were never met, we will no longer be denying that part of ourselves. When we embrace those weaknesses of need (they are not weaknesses of character!), we are embracing that part of us that was pushed aside and we can be embraced by God's love (see Chapter Nine).

❖ The process of restoration will take time, and a healthy church is one of the best places for the process to take place. God will use people in His church to be instruments of His love, and involvement in His body will help us look to God as our life source.

And God is our life source. He gives us His truth to live by, and He offers us the gracious gift of His redemptive love. Scripture tells us that God's plan is that we be redeemed and that we become the people God designed us to be (Eph. 4:15). Scripture also invites us to experience the new creation and the new birth through which we are transformed into the image of His Son Jesus Christ (2 Cor. 3:18).

My prayer for you is that you will receive a love for God's truth and that you will respond to God's grace by turning to Him as Lord of your life.

## *Your Own Story*

- *What did you learn about God as you read about His truth?*
- *What was the most interesting thing you learned about yourself when you read about how you are created in God's image?*
- *Spend some time in prayer, asking God to re-parent you in the area(s) where you suspect or are aware of unmet childhood needs.*

## God's Image/Our Being and Sense of Self

| | | |
|---|---|---|
| **Needs:** | Touch | To explore their world |
| | Warmth | To develop boundaries |
| | Nurture | To trust parents completely |

**Unmet When . . .**

"You don't exist."
"You are unimportant."
"You aren't wanted."
"We wanted a child of the opposite sex."
"Hurry up!"
Parents' unrealistic expectations
Unloving facial expressions

**Possible Consequences:**

Addictions (drugs, alcohol, sex)
Obesity
Emotional dependency
Performance orientation
Doing what others want/nonassertiveness
Lack of creativity
Fear of taking initiative

## God's Likeness/Our Sense of Order and Sexual Identity

**Needs:**

To develop social relationships
To recognize gender differences
To test power

**Unmet When . . .**

Lack of bonding with either parent
Abuse (sexual, physical, or emotional)
Nurturing needs are linked to sexuality

**Possible Consequences:**

Lack of proper gender identity
Lack of clear role in relationships
Seeking mothering or fathering through sexual contacts
Lack of boundaries
Failure to respect authority

## God's Dominion/Our Sense of Purpose and Dominion

| | |
|---|---|
| Needs: | To learn how to learn<br>To develop skills<br>To learn to think logically<br>To identify inherent abilities |
| Unmet When . . . | Lack of modeling<br>Abandonment |
| Possible Consequences: | Inferiority complex<br>Passivity<br>Overachiever |

CHAPTER ❦ FIVE

# Exchanging Truth for a Lie

*I needed help. I knew that, on my own, I couldn't always identify when my system of deception was working, so I asked my wife to become my partner in my restoration. Helen learned when and how to ask me what my real motives were in certain situations, and this greatly helped me understand my patterns of addiction. I began to see how I exchanged truth for a lie and how my patterns of addictive behavior worked in my life. My human pride made it hard to acknowledge my motives, admit the deception I was living, confess these actions as sin, and replace the lies I had long believed with God's freeing truth. My recovery, however, depended on those steps.*

Just as important as receiving God's saving grace is receiving the threefold truth about His image, His likeness, and His dominion, truth which has significant implications for who we are and how we are to live. Even if a childhood of unmet needs made us unable to recognize these truths for many years, we can now receive God's truth and let it serve as the solid foundation for our life. If we don't, we must accept responsibility for choosing to suppress the truth about God and about who He created us to be.

Satan, however, is the vigilant father of lies, and he does what he can to turn us away from God's truth. In fact, all of our sin patterns are based on a lie, based on a fiction that we use to suppress the truth about how God wants us to live (Rom. 1:18). The word *suppress* means "to hold down," and people living in a sin pattern have suppressed the truth about God and its implications for them personally. But suppressing the truth is like trying to hold a balloon under water—both the balloon and the truth will keep trying to resurface despite our efforts to push them down.

Working against our efforts and Satan's efforts to suppress God's truth is the Holy Spirit. One of His roles in the lives of believers is to convict us of the lies in our life and show us God's truth. Furthermore, the apostle Paul teaches that God's eternal power and divine nature are obvious in nature and that we therefore have no excuse for not knowing the truth about God that is revealed in His creation (Rom. 1:20). To act against God's truth, we must violate our conscience.

And we act against God's truth when we act in opposition to the fact that we are created in His image, in His likeness, and to share in His dominion. Since Jesus is the truth (John 14:6), any behavior of ours which is a variation from His character—His patience, kindness, humility, love, righteousness—is a distortion and a lie. And any belief we have that disputes God's goodness, power, love, righteousness, and justice is also a distortion and a lie. And such false beliefs lie behind our seductive systems of addiction.

## The Origin of Systems of Addiction

A system of addiction is a lifestyle of wrong actions based on false ideas or wrong thoughts which we adopted in an attempt to have our needs met or to protect ourselves from being hurt again. Whatever system we develop for having our needs met is an attempt to find wholeness and healing from wounds in our childhood. Since every human being naturally longs for home and for good parenting from a loving mother and father, it is often at precisely this point that we are easily sabotaged. We can mistakenly set out on a path which seems to lead to love and life and not realize that it actually leads to death.

We may also act out our feelings of loss inappropriately by blaming others for our situation or acting angrily toward those people (parents, siblings, friends, religious leaders, or others) who did not meet our needs or fulfill our expectations. Our anger as well as our sorrow about our unmet needs can develop into an attitude of bitter judgment. We may, for instance, find ourselves acting on the desire to see another person hurt in the same way that we have been hurt. Such actions are caused by a lack of forgiveness and our failure to respond to God's grace.

Hebrews 12:15 states, "See to it that no one comes short of the grace of God; that no root of bitterness springing up causes trouble, and by it many be defiled." When bitterness does spring up, that feeling may extend beyond people to God Himself. Why did God let a certain situation happen? He could have prevented it, but He didn't—so how can I ask Him to meet my needs now? At this point we have redirected our bitterness away from those people who have let us down; we have transferred our bitter feelings to God. And we can not honor any person or God whom we have deemed weak.

Neither can we give thanks to God. Unfulfilled expectations—whether a lack of love, financial insecurity, unhappiness with our physical appearance, a wrong sexual preference, a rape, one's heritage—lead to an ungrateful attitude. Bitter judgments alienate us from God and other people and result in feelings of abandonment and loneliness. Once our heart has become bitter against God, we develop a system of living by which we attempt to meet our needs on our own. We exchange His truth for a lie and turn away from His will for our lives.

## Lies behind the System: Lies about God

Behind every system of wrong behavior is a series of lies we believe about God and His character. The Garden dialogue between Satan and Eve exemplifies this kind of lie (Gen. 3:1-5) (a chart at the end of this chapter summarizes these untruths).

❖ Lie #1: Twisting God's words, Satan says to Eve, "Indeed, has God said, 'You shall not eat from any tree of the garden'?" (Gen. 3:1). With this question, Satan implies that God will not meet Eve's basic needs and, second, that the limitations which God has set will limit Eve's well-being. Today, we still too easily accept those implications as truth. We wonder whether or not God will meet our basic needs; we wonder whether we can trust Him. We tell ourselves that God didn't in the past and that, in the present, God can't, God won't, or maybe He just isn't.

❖ Lie #2: After Eve misquotes God's instruction, Satan responds, "You surely shall not die [if you eat from the tree or touch it]!" (Gen. 3:4). Here, Satan wrongly suggests that there are no consequences—either long-range or short-term—when we make choices that violate God's Word or His will. When we, like Eve, begin to believe this (and the belief that our secret actions have no consequences is fundamental to our denial), we begin to live a life out of touch with reality.

❖ Lie #3: Satan suggests that God didn't want Eve to eat from the tree because "in the day you eat from it your eyes will be opened, and you will be like God, knowing good and evil" (Gen. 3:5). Satan builds on Lie #1 by suggesting that, if our basic needs are not going to be met by God, we must become our own god and work to meet our needs ourselves. We find this lie especially easy to believe if we learned not to trust our parents and, by extension, God our heavenly Father.

Let me add that bitterness against God can contribute to our acceptance of this third lie, and that bitterness can have its roots in comparisons we make between ourselves and other people. When we decide that we have been shortchanged in life, we feel jealous and envious of others and, in our faulty reasoning, we conclude that if we are to ever get what we deserve, we must do it ourselves and in our own way. This results in selfish ambition which has a disregard for God, His kingdom, and other people. This disregard widens the gap between us and God.

Think about your system of addiction. Have you built it on one of these lies about God? Have you believed that God is either unable or unwilling to meet your needs? Were you convinced that there will be no consequences for your actions? Or that, if you're going to have your needs met, you have to meet those needs yourself?

## Lies behind the System: Lies about Self

Perhaps you're believing lies about yourself as well as lies about God. Once we develop a faulty belief system about God, a faulty belief system about ourselves develops. Our faulty belief systems can begin as early as birth and continue on in us until they are intercepted by God. Consider this system of lies many wounded people believe about themselves (see the chart at the end of this chapter).

❖ Lie #1: "No one would love me if they really knew me." Many wounded people feel that they can't measure up to God's expectations or to other people's expectations. I remember people telling me that they were blessed by my sermons. Although their words always encouraged me, I had a gut-level feeling of disbelief, and I always wondered if they would be able to love and accept me if they knew about my inward struggles. We may doubt God's love for us in the same way we can doubt the love and acceptance of other people.

But we can counter Lie #1 with Romans 5:8 which says, "God demonstrates His own love toward us, in that while we were yet sinners, Christ died for us." We can believe the truth and learn to rest in God's love for us.

❖ Lie #2: "I am unworthy and undeserving of love." People who believe this lie often struggle when blessings come and they experience success. Their low self-esteem makes them feel quite undeserving of any blessing, and that poor self-image can cause them to misunderstand God's grace. They see God's grace as something to be earned rather than a free gift. Gifts are hard to receive when we feel unworthy of the attention.

Ephesians 1:3 counters Lie #2—"Blessed be the God and Father of our Lord Jesus Christ, who has blessed us with every spiritual blessing in the heavenly places in Christ." None of us deserves the blessings God bestows. All we can do is receive them and thank Him, knowing that any merit on our part comes only through Jesus Christ. And, after all, our standing in Jesus Christ is yet another gift from God!

❖ Lie #3: "If I don't meet my needs, they will never be met." This lie about ourselves mirrors Lie #3 about God, and we are acting on this lie when we start to meet an unmet need in an unhealthy or sinful way. Sex, alcohol, drugs, or rage can seem to offer relief for our pain, but that source of relief—that means we have chosen to take care of our needs on our own—soon becomes the most important thing in our life.

We can again let the truth of God's Word counter Lie #3. In Philippians 4:19 we read, "And my God shall supply all your needs according to His riches in glory in Christ Jesus."

It is foolish to act against God's truth, but often we do. We become easy prey for Satan's lies about God and lies about us. In Scripture we are warned, "There is a way which seems right to a man, but its end is the way of death" (Prov. 16:25). We need to cling to God's truth and so avoid the way of death outlined by these lies.

## A Limited Perspective

These lies about God and about ourselves fuel "bitter jealousy and selfish ambition" and result in a "wisdom" that is "earthly, natural, demonic" (James 3:14-15).

❖ First, this belief system which discounts God's power and love limits our view of time and space to this sphere alone. We are not able to see beyond the earthly realm to the spiritual realm and eternity. Often we will not consider five or ten years from now, much less the end of this life and what happens then. We have a focus that is limited to the here and now.

❖ Second, James writes, believing lies results in a perspective that is natural or unspiritual. We make decisions and plans without spiritual sensitivity or even spiritual concern. We act as if we are masters of our own destiny, accountable to no one. Professing to be wise, we become fools (Rom. 1:22).

❖ Finally, our thinking becomes demonized. We notice that our plans and the systems that we have devised to take care of ourselves seem to work out unusually well. We also notice that, once our system is functioning, the number of coincidental opportunities to use that system is almost diabolical. As many former sex addicts have told me, Satan seems to set up an amazing number of chances for people to satisfy their addiction. The demonization of our thinking also causes us to feel overwhelmed by an exaggerated need to act out our system and satisfy our addiction. Finally, diabolical schemes and a diabolical empowerment to fulfill those schemes may accompany the fulfillment of our corrupt desires.

Behind the earthly, natural, and even demonized wisdom that can lead to a system of addiction is a very human motivation: we desire to be complete. And we are motivated to strive for that goal of completeness by either a fear of pain or a desire for pleasure.

❖ A fear of pain, loss, failure, rejection, abandonment, or death will motivate us to develop a system of protection for ourselves. We fear that some kind of loss would leave us incomplete, so we try to prevent that by our systems of defense.

❖ The desire for pleasure, gain, fulfillment, success, security, and survival can also motivate us to develop a certain system of behavior. We want to be complete and content, but we choose an unhealthy means to that acceptable goal.

These drives toward completion are legitimate in God's order and purpose as related to His kingdom. For example, it isn't wrong to fear loss or pain. In fact, fear—specifically, the fear of hell or God's wrath—can motivate us to avoid sin. Neither is it wrong to desire God's glory for others and for ourselves. In fact, God's glory is the ultimate type of pleasure we human beings can desire and the ultimate loss we human beings can fear. Our Lord said, "Seek first His kingdom and His righteousness; and all these things shall be added to you" (Matt. 6:33). However, when we believe Satan's lies about God and ourselves, our desire to avoid pain or to find fulfillment are no longer godly drives. Instead they become "earthly, natural, [and] demonic" (James 3:15); they become the basis of very self-centered reasoning.

## Trying to Meet Our Needs

All of us have systems we rely on at times, especially when we feel lonely, angry, tired, or rejected after our needs for identity, order and belonging, and purpose (God's image, likeness, or dominion) have not been met. At those times, we may attempt to fulfill our needs in various wrong ways. Motivated by either the fear of pain/loss or the desire for pleasure/fulfillment, we will try to avoid pain by going into isolation and withdrawing or we will develop a system of behavior to help us meet our needs in an illegitimate way (see the chart at the end of this chapter).

### *God's Image: Our Sense of Being and Identity*

We may develop systems to find the kind of nurturing we didn't receive as children, the kind of nurturing that gives children a sense of being and worth.

❖ People who fear loss may avoid intimacy and nurturing by developing a system in which they either don't allow people to get close to them or they sabotage close relationships. My system worked that way. Often when people tried to be close to me, I sabotaged the relationship; I rejected them before they could reject me. The fear of pain outweighed the possible enjoyment I might have found in the relationship, so, for the most part, I avoided intimacy altogether.

❖ Limited relationships based on business, sports, or special interests are another way of avoiding intimacy. Motivated by our fear of being rejected or abandoned, we don't allow ourselves to share our hearts. Furthermore, we may cover up that fear of rejection and abandonment with alcohol, drugs, work, or some other addiction.

❖ Some people are motivated more by pleasure than fear, and these people—whose basic needs were also not met when they were children—will develop emotionally dependent relationships. They will either be dependent on others, or they'll manipulate others to be dependent on them.

❖ A man whose life was characterized by bitter hurt and painful emptiness came to see me. A very handsome young man, John had had relationship after relationship with various women. He also shared with me that many families in the congregation had become like parents to him. How did this happen? And why was it the source of such emptiness?

The pattern of John's behavior was clear. He would immediately share his needs with people he was attracted to. When those people had a need to take care of people, they quickly became emotionally involved. John used his system of emotional manipulation to seduce people into taking care of him and to feel good about meeting his needs. He would go from woman to woman and family to family, leaving behind broken hearts and fractured relationships.

Despite the number of people who cared about him, John was still empty because he was trying to fulfill an insatiable childhood need through people. This effort always leads to disappointment and disillusionment because, although God may use people to help us along the road to restoration, only God Himself can meet those needs we've had since childhood.

Eventually, John came to understand his system. He realized that God alone could meet his deepest longings for love. He also let go of the system that he had relied on for so long and changed his approach to relationships. Now John is in a maturing marriage relationship, and he is growing in his own Christian walk.

❖ Our need for the nurturing, approval, and acceptance we didn't receive as children can lead to various sexual experiences. A minister, for example, shared with me how he was often attracted to people who admired him. In fact, Gerald always made himself especially available to counsel the women who admired him. He admitted to me that his attraction to these women was inappropriate and that he would experience an emotional high and look forward to each session like a fix.

Following a counseling session, there was always a quick hug which, in later sessions, became a prolonged hug. He would then begin to share his marital problems and how his own needs were not being met. The sessions would eventually conclude with him sexually acting out his frustrations. Afterward he would be filled with feelings of shame, disgust, and isolation. When he first shared his experience with me, he said that the encounters "just happened," but I knew—and Gerald knew—that wasn't the case. There is always a system behind an ongoing pattern of behavior.

After multiple affairs, Gerald's behavior was exposed. Through the loving discipline of some Christian leaders in his own church, Gerald was restored in personal wholeness, to his place within his family, and to a ministry.

### *God's Likeness: Our Need for Order and Belonging*

In our quest for a sense of order and belonging in our life, we may once again be motivated by our fear of pain or our desire for pleasure.

❖ We can deal with this pain by rejecting our gender identity. Alan told me that he never knew his natural father. When Alan's mother remarried after his natural father had left her, his stepfather rejected him. When his mother married a third time, this father not only rejected Alan but also emotionally and physically abused him. Alan's older brother, however, was a favorite of the stepfather, and the two of them didn't want Alan around because, in their words, he was too young. Treated like this, Alan began to develop a hatred and distrust for men. At the same time, he closely identified with his mother, having learned feminine characteristics and skills for the home. Alan finally rejected the gender God had given him.

One day in my office, Alan began to understand what he was doing, and right before my eyes his voice and his facial expressions changed. His speech lost some of the feminine characteristics he had adopted. This counseling session wasn't a case of a quick fix, but it was the beginning of a restoration process that unfolded over several years. During that time, Alan learned to enter into wholesome relationships with other men, and he learned to accept his identity as a man.

❖ Another way people deal with the fear of loss in relationship is to simply isolate themselves from relationships with other people. If people don't get to know us, the reasoning goes, then they'll never know our deep insecurity about our gender or about being in relationship with other people. We can also deal with rejection by rejecting other people first. This can become our unhealthy way of dealing with the need to belong.

❖ When we are motivated by pleasure to try to fulfill this need to belong, we often exaggerate our sexuality. How well I remember Doug as he stood before the other members of the men's Bible study and shared how he had exaggerated about his hunting trips, athletic abilities, and business achievements. But as Doug shared, he began to sob. Several of the men put their arms around him and offered him comfort in his pain. Later Doug told me that it was a relief to lay aside his system of lies. He also saw that God was giving him the acceptance he had tried to gain by lying. This was the beginning of Doug's freedom. The struggle not to exaggerate continues, but Doug is on the road to restoration.

Doug had learned his system of exaggeration (or lies) from his childhood efforts to get people to accept him. But being the macho hero in his stories was a perversion of his masculinity and a rejection of the tenderness and gentleness that should also be part of a male's life.

❖ Just as men exaggerate their masculinity, women exaggerate their femininity through dress and attitude and stifle such qualities as decision-making abilities or financial insight that are good but not, in their minds, feminine.

❖ To fulfill our desire to belong, we may also associate with people we admire. As we strive to belong, we may find ourselves consistently doing more than expected. We may constantly try to please other people. In our system, our sense of belonging is very much performance-oriented.

### *God's Dominion: Purpose and Dominion*

We may develop systems to give us a sense of purpose and fulfill our sense of personal dominion. Once again, fear of pain and desire for pleasure can motivate us.

❖ Our fear of pain may make us passive: We don't want to hurt again, so we don't try to accomplish anything for fear of failing or being rejected.

❖ We let others make decisions. I saw this tendency in me. I didn't feel worthy to make decisions—who was I to have an opinion? Besides, when I let others make decisions, I wouldn't fail. This avoidance of decisions made me very passive. When I took my car to the mechanic and it wasn't fixed properly, I'd pay the bill—and then take it to another mechanic. Besides not wanting to make decisions, I didn't have the ability to confront people. It was less painful not to confront. I was motivated by a fear of pain as well as fear of failure.

❖ When people are motivated by pleasure, they can become over-achievers in their quest for purpose. They may aggressively defend their own boundaries and overstep the boundaries of others. In their efforts to meet their need for dominion, they become a human *doing* instead of human *being*.

## Roles As Well As Systems

Just like the systems we develop to protect us from hurt, the roles that we assume in our family, peer group, business, and even church become a way to avoid pain and meet our needs.

### *Roles Placed on Us*

Many of these roles, however, are not freely assumed. Instead they are placed on us by the people around us.

❖ Consider how people's words give us roles. How many of us are living out roles given to us by others? Some people, for instance, have been identified as the smart one since grade school. As a child, I got a lot of attention by making good grades in school, and that kind of approval has been one of the driving forces in my life.

❖ Other people may have been the scapegoat in the family. Even though that role is shaming and painful, it is familiar, so the scapegoat may hang on to it.

❖ Never will I forget the painful expression on Sean's face when he came to see me. He had begun visiting adult bookstores and acting out some homosexual activity. He said that he couldn't understand his behavior; it seemed so foreign to him. I knew right away that this could be a system Sean developed because of certain unmet needs, but there seemed to be further reasons for his behavior. What was the lie that he believed?

As we talked, I asked him if there had ever been a time when he had been deeply shamed or embarrassed by someone. Was he perhaps living out a name he had been called? He then told me about the time when he was in the junior-high locker room and an older athlete called him a fag. Suddenly there was deathly silence as everyone stopped and listened. When I asked Sean how he had felt when this happened, I saw him make a tight fist. He told me that he was angry and wanted to hit the older boy, but he knew that if he did, he would be beaten up and even more embarrassed.

I then asked Sean how he felt now, and he again said that he was angry. Because of other circumstances in his life, Sean had begun to believe the lie the older boy had spoken in jest, and Sean had lived with that powerful word until it became a raging fire that set the course of his life. In times of loneliness and doubt, he began to believe that maybe he did want to be homosexual. He began to experiment, all the while feeling deeply sad and not really wanting to take part in the homosexual lifestyle. Believing a lie, he was miserable. Like Sean, many people—and maybe you're one of them—are affected by jokes and sarcastic remarks that derail the truth and so reset the course of their life.

Sean, however, was able to see the power of the spoken word. He came to understand how he had been acting out the anger he had felt in junior high school. When he realized he was acting out of feelings and not being who he really was, he released his anger and sorrow to the Lord and, through Christ, experienced an inward change in his identity. This inward change resulted in significant changes in his behavior. Sean had found freedom from a powerful word and a path to restoration.

*Role Reversal*

❖ The family can also be the scene of role reversal. A young church leader, for instance, had ruined his ministry when he had started getting involved with different young women every place he went. Ed's involvement was not motivated by the desire for sexual fulfillment alone; instead he was acting out of hate and anger dating back to his youth. He explained to me how his father was an alcoholic and his mother could not deal with her emotions. Incapacitated, she became bedfast, and Ed became the surrogate husband. During his teen years, Ed never felt that he could date. In fact, he felt guilty even having friends. All the while, his mother shared openly the problems and faults concerning her husband.

It was important for Ed to understand the role reversal within his family and that he was not responsible for it. Sadly, he had lost his childhood, but he now realized that he was not responsible for having become the husband. He had been put into a role that God never intended him to have.

As a result of ongoing counseling with professional Christian therapists, Ed was able to let go of the role he had been forced to play. Today, Ed is happily married, successful in his job, active in his church, and seeking the role in ministry he believes God has for him.

❖ A child may become an extension of the mother or the father. Perhaps the father wanted to enter a certain profession but never did, so he forced his child into that role. The child may be living out a parent's dream of being an athlete, minister, or doctor, a dream that was never realized. Parents become stuck in the dreams of their youth and the needs of their childhood and, as adults, try to fulfill those dreams through their children.

❖ One role that we may have assumed is the victim role. Victims set themselves up for this role by seeking out abusive people and experiencing the same kind of damaging results they knew before. By doing this, they continue to live out the victim role.

## Understanding a System of Addiction

A big step towards dismantling our system of addiction is to identify our systems as well as any roles we are playing. As I stated at the beginning of the chapter, a system of addiction is a lifestyle of wrong actions based on false ideas or wrong thoughts which we adopted in an attempt to have our needs met or to protect ourselves from being hurt again.

The New Testament teaches that when darkness is brought to light, it becomes light (Eph. 5:13). When I began to discover my own systems of behavior, I brought them into the light of the Lord Jesus by confessing them to Christ as well as to trusted friends and a mature Christian counselor. Sometimes the problems were solved (I took certain actions and made a conscious effort to stop the system), and sometimes the problems just dissolved (recognizing the temptation or pattern somehow robbed it of its power over me). Darkness brought to light becomes light. Once we see our system for what it is and recognize the falsehood it is based on, then we can lay it aside.

During my own process of restoration, I had to look very closely at my systems of addiction. I had been seduced by the lie that a certain system of actions would restore and repair the wounds of my childhood. This system, however, became a way for me to control and manipulate others so that they would fulfill my needs for closeness. Helen helped me see, for instance, how I would develop a relationship with a person who needed me. This person's dependence, though, was actually meeting my need to be close to someone who needed me. Seeing this was an important step of recovery, an important step toward living as God would have me live.

Lies about God and about ourselves which we accept as truth and childhood needs for nurturing, relationship, and purpose—all of these contribute to the systems of the flesh we use to take care of ourselves. Unless our system of addiction is intercepted and dealt with by the power of the Holy Spirit, we will continue in decline to the point of spiritual bankruptcy. Our system will become the focus of our life, and we will feel isolated from God and removed from His love and care. But by claiming the truth of God's Word—truth which proclaims His love for us and His promises to care for us—we can release the lies we've believed and, with the power of the Holy Spirit, work on building a healthier way of life.

## Your Own Story

- *Which lie about God do you find easiest to believe? Find a Scripture that counters this lie with a biblical truth, and commit that verse to memory.*
- *Which lie about yourself do you find easiest to believe? Commit to memory the Scriptural response provided, or find another verse which will strengthen you in the truth and memorize it.*
- *What roles have been forced on you and/or what role reversal have you experienced in life? Write out a statement describing who you are and what is freeing you from these false roles.*

## A Faulty Belief System about God

Lie #1 *"You shall not eat from any tree of the garden"* (Gen. 3:1).

- God is not able to meet our basic needs.
- God will not meet our basic needs.
- The limitations God has set will limit our well-being.

Lie #2 *"You surely shall not die!"* (Gen. 3:4).

There are no consequences—either long-range or short-term—when we make choices which violate God's Word and His will for us.

Lie #3 *"You will be like God, knowing good and evil"* (Gen. 3:5).

If our basic needs are going to be met, we must become our own god and work to meet our needs ourselves.

## A Faulty Belief System about Ourselves

Lie #1 *"No one would love me if they really knew me."*

The Truth: "God demonstrates His own love toward us, in that while we were yet sinners, Christ died for us."—Romans 5:8

Lie #2 *"I am unworthy and undeserving of love."*

The Truth: "Blessed be the God and Father of our Lord Jesus Christ, who has blessed us with every spiritual blessing in the heavenly places in Christ."—Ephesians 1:3

Lie #3 *"If I don't meet my needs, they will never be met."*

The Truth: "My God shall supply all your needs according to His riches in glory in Christ Jesus."—Philippians 4:19

## Living Out Lies

When God's truth about who we are has been suppressed and replaced with a lie, we may live out the lie in various ways.

### God's Image/Our Being and Sense of Self

Motivated by Fear of Pain, We . . .
- Avoid intimacy and nurturing by not allowing close relationships
- Avoid intimacy and nurturing by sabotaging relationships
- Build limited relationships around business, sports, hobbies
- Cover up our pain with our addiction (alcohol, drugs, work, etc.)

Motivated by Desire for Pleasure, We . . .
- Develop emotionally dependent relationships
- Manipulate others to be dependent on us
- Engage in sexual activities
- Feed our feelings by eating

### God's Likeness/Our Sense of Order and Sexual Identity

Motivated by Fear of Pain, We . . .
- Reject our gender identity
- Isolate ourselves from relationships
- Avoid rejection by rejecting others first

Motivated by Desire for Pleasure, We . . .
- Exaggerate our maleness or femaleness
- Seek our identity through others
- Strive to belong

### God's Dominion/Our Sense of Purpose and Dominion

Motivated by Fear of Pain, We . . .
- Are passive
- Let others make decisions
- Are nonconfrontive and unassertive

Motivated by Desire for Pleasure, We . . .
- Are overaggressive
- Are overachievers
- Become a human doing instead of a human being

CHAPTER ❦ SIX

# Our Systems As Addictions

*The soft-spoken counselor looked me squarely in the eyes. Her words were not what I had expected to hear. Slowly and deliberately, she said, "Don, you're an addict." In the quiet of the room, her words pierced my heart like a sword. The word "addict" was a dark and awful word that I associated with alcoholics and skid-row bums, with heroin users and people going nowhere. To admit to myself that I was an addict—that was something I did not want to do.*

I was nervous as Helen and I drove the three-and-a-half hours to visit the psychotherapist who had been recommended to us. I wasn't convinced that she could help where others hadn't been able to. As I entered Sharon's office, she greeted me with sparkling eyes and a confidence that communicated God's presence and His love. I was still nervous when I sat down, and I was wondering what would transpire from this.

Memories of previous counseling sessions flooded my mind. I remembered my third session with a psychiatrist. I was feeling guilty for even being there—I must not be trusting God enough or I wouldn't be sitting in this office! Then I noticed that the psychiatrist, who wasn't saying anything, had struck an unusual posture. He was leaning back in his chair with his eyes closed. Not familiar with psychiatric techniques, I wasn't sure how to respond. Was he trying to help me get in touch with my anger by pretending to ignore me? Then he began to snore, hardly an encouragement for me to say more. Anger welled up in me as I walked out of the room never to return.

Then there was the Christian priest known for counseling people involved in sexual perversion. Even though I was afraid of the events that could unfold if my secret world became known, I made an appointment with him. As I sat in his office and shared my story, he looked me in the eyes and told me that he had the same problem! He offered some safeguards he was using and cautioned me to be careful so that I wouldn't be exposed and my ministry ruined. From that point, I heard nothing that he said. I knew that he couldn't help me if he couldn't help himself.

## A Sword of Truth

Now here I was in Sharon's office, full of doubt that anyone would be able to help me. I knew that Sharon had helped a friend of mine who had struggled with a problem similar to mine, but I wondered if she could help me. Questions filled my mind, but Sharon immediately put me at ease.

As I began my story, I was relieved and pleased that Sharon was not judgmental. I shared with her the exposure of my secret world and all the loss that I had experienced in my life as a result. Sharon was very gracious and attentive, and I began to feel that she'd be able to help me with my anger and depression. At that moment, I decided that I'd stick with this therapy no matter how long it took (it ended up taking about a year-and-a-half).

As hope sprang up in me, I began to share details of my past behavior. That was when Sharon looked right at me and told me that I was an addict. The sound of that word—that powerful, awful word—hung in the air. It seemed to me that Sharon could have described my situation some other way. Couldn't we say that I was unable to overcome certain temptations in my life? Deep in my heart, though, I knew that Sharon was right. I had stepped into a world of emotional and sexual addiction. Although I had stopped acting out, I was still powerless over my addiction, and I needed the grace of God.

In 2 Timothy 2, Paul instructs Timothy to gently correct those who need it so that "God may grant them repentance leading to the knowledge of the truth, and they may come to their senses and escape from the snare of the devil, having been held captive by him to do his will" (2:25-26). These verses offered me hope that I could be delivered from my addiction. Still, the word *addict* was frightening, even after I learned that many people have an addiction in their life.

## What Is an Addiction?

When our system becomes our reason for living—our life source—or the very basis of our identity, we are in a stage of addiction.

❖ Addiction is a compulsive and repetitive act that has life-damaging consequences.

❖ Webster's says that the verb *addict* means "to devote or surrender (oneself) to something habitually or obsessively."

❖ Addiction involves a felt loss of choice. An addiction limits our ability to choose; the compulsion limits our choice.

❖ An addiction is a way of acting out feelings we have not been able to express.

❖ Acting on an addiction is a mood-altering experience. When we haven't learned to deal with certain emotions, for instance, we may develop a system to alter those feelings. Whenever we experience the feelings we can't handle, we will do something to try to cover them up or change them.

❖ Spiritually, an addiction is a form of idolatry. Our addiction becomes our god, the focus of our life.

❖ Addiction is a compulsion, obsession, and preoccupation that enslaves a person's will and desire.

❖ The means of satisfying an addiction is a fix or high.

❖ Preoccupation and fantasy are aspects of the addiction.

## Identifying an Addiction

Dr. Gerald May, author of *Addiction and Grace,* identifies five characteristics of addiction, and as I read about them, I realized that Dr. May was describing me (see the chart at the end of this chapter).

1. The Need for More—Addicts have attached their unmet needs to something or someone until that thing or person becomes the reason for living. As a result, addicts want more of that thing or person. Also, when we are involved in our addiction, we feel more creative and alive—even though our addiction may destroy us—and, again, we want more of whatever we are addicted to.

2. Withdrawal Symptoms or Symptoms of Stress—The second characteristic of an addiction is the stress caused by being without whatever we are addicted to, whether it be drugs, sex, food, or something else.

3. Deception—The third characteristic of an addiction is actually *self*-deception. We will often justify our acts by saying that we don't have a problem or that we can stop our behavior whenever we want to. We are living the lie that we don't have a problem. As I have already mentioned, part of my self-deception was not acknowledging that I had a problem. I separated my problem from me the person. I was in denial.

4. A Loss of Willpower—With an addiction comes a loss of willpower. We will try to go without our addiction, yet we eventually fail. Even when we vow to God that we will never do it again, we fall. Our willpower is short-lived at best.

5. Distortion of Attention—When our addiction becomes the center of our life, we experience a distortion of attention. The addiction becomes the reason for our existence, and we schedule our lives around our addiction. I have talked to men who have spent enormous amounts of money on their addiction and even lost their jobs because their attention was so caught up in their addiction.

## The Path to Addiction

In previous chapters, I have outlined the process that leads to addiction:

❖ The first step towards addiction is the suppression of the truth that we were created in God's image, in His likeness, and to share in His dominion. Whenever this truth about us is suppressed, we find ourselves suppressing the truth about God. Ignoring the truth that we were created in God's image and its implications for our lives, we become a distortion of God's image.

❖ Second, we become bitter and judgmental. When we have experienced sorrows, hurts, disappointments, and unfulfilled expectations at the hands of those who were to meet our needs, we turn against God in bitter judgment.

❖ Third, we develop a wrong belief system. Our false ideas about God and our false ideas about ourselves lead us to abandon God's commandments and desires for our life. Instead, we act on our own to see to it that our needs are met.

❖ Finally, we develop a wrong value system. Having begun to live life according to our rules, our values no longer reflect God's plan for our life. We are not living for His glory or His kingdom; we are living for ourselves.

## Objects of Addiction

Not living for God means living for ourselves and searching for value, purpose, significance, and even something to worship in another person, activity, or philosophy. Not living for God means, in the words of the apostle Paul, exchanging "the glory of the incorruptible God for an image in the form of corruptible man and of birds and four-footed animals and crawling creatures" (Rom. 1:23). This verse seems to accurately outline four major types of addiction. "Corruptible man" points to a people addiction, an unhealthy emotional dependency on others, a humanistic philosophy, and even the elevation of athletics to a form of worship. "Birds" represent pride in our intellectualism (I used to read several books a week to cover up my pain) as well as the pursuit of social prestige and false mysticism. "Four-footed animals" represent an addiction to power, money, and position. Finally, "crawling creatures" are symbolic of sexual addiction, black and white magic, satanism, hedonism, the filthy, and the crude.

Having listed the idols (and an addiction is an idol) which human beings choose over God, Paul then describes the downward addictive cycle. After a person has stepped into a wrong value system, he or she will tend to use rather than honor other people (Rom. 1:24-25). Instead of reaching out to others, our own addiction becomes the focus of our existence, and we look at other people in terms of how we can use them to meet our needs. Instead of having God's love for people, we have a lust to use people.

The next step after this people addiction is sexual addiction (Rom. 1:26-27). An addict's sexual needs become the most important thing in life. An addict's life revolves around sexual need rather than God's commands. Again, people are regarded as the means to the fulfillment of an addiction rather than fellow heirs to God's kingdom.

Paul then warns about where these people who are living for themselves are headed. He describes how they will be "filled with all unrighteousness, wickedness, greed, evil; full of envy, murder, strife, deceit, malice . . . haters of God, insolent, arrogant, boastful, inventors of evil . . . without understanding, untrustworthy, unloving, unmerciful" (Rom. 1:29-31).

It is obvious that one should experience guilt and shame after such behavior, but if a person has an addiction, consequences are not considered and conscience is unheeded. Addicts really do have an unrealistic world view, and in that world view, there is a wrong appraisal of actions and an inversion of good and evil (Rom. 1:32). Wrong becomes right and right, wrong. At this point, addicts probably don't recognize that they need help; nor would they want it.

This kind of blindness to one's need for help will not be changed by reasoning, threats, or pleas. What can help is prayer, and it is important to pray for addicted people who can not see that their lifestyle is wrong. We must pray that the Holy Spirit will break through their mindset so that they can hear the truth. We can pray that the Lord will bring circumstances into their life so that they will see their lifestyle for the idolatrous and destructive thing it is. We can pray that God will help them break denial. And we must pray that the Lord will lead an addicted person to repentance.

## Addictive Relationships

People can also be the object of our addiction (see Chapter Ten). This kind of inappropriate bonding and emotional dependence happen when we:

❖ Look to someone else as the ultimate source of purpose, help, or even survival.

❖ Begin to drop or neglect other relationships to spend time with that person.

❖ Become more concerned with the well-being of the addictive relationship than our own immediate family members.

❖ Note an element of sensuality and focus on the feelings and the fantasies of being together rather than on God's work.

❖ Discuss, reciprocate, and therefore energize the soul-bonding.

❖ Need to be with the other person often. The relationship becomes exclusive rather than inclusive.

❖ Think about the other person constantly. The almost-constant state of togetherness binds the souls together.

## Red Flags for Sexual Addiction

Addictions—whatever the type—don't come on suddenly. Most of them have red-flag warnings built in to warn us that we are on the way to destruction. One red flag for sexual addiction, for instance, is an interest in pornography. Do you visit the wrong type of bookstores or read the wrong magazines? Another red flag is involvement in affairs—not one affair, but many affairs that follow a pattern and become a cycle. Another red flag is compulsive masturbation. There may be consistent sexual innuendos. A red flag can be flirtation and trying to get people to respond to us. There may be cruising and denying where we are because we are out looking for sexual adventure. These red flags need to be heeded if the downward cycle of addiction is to be avoided.

## Taking Responsibility

If we are involved in an addiction, we will need help coming out of it. I know from experience that we cannot do it alone. I also know that an important step toward coming out of an addiction is understanding that we are responsible for our addiction even if we feel that, at this point, we are beyond choice.

We must take responsibility for our addiction because we chose our addiction through a fourfold process. First, there was experimentation and the discovery that the object of our soon-to-be-addiction made us feel better. Second, we sought out those same feelings of relief and pleasure. Also, fantasy became part of the high: getting there was part of the excitement and pleasure. Third, we developed an obsession for feeling good by means of our addiction. We also experienced some difficulty in finding the relief and pleasure we initially received from our addiction. Fourth, our addiction started to consume our time, our energy, and our thoughts until it took its place as the focus of our existence. Our addiction became our world and the basis for our now-distorted reality.

At each of these four steps, I had chosen my addiction and now, like anyone who has an addiction, I had to face the responsibility of having done so. Facing that responsibility becomes increasingly more difficult. (A chart at the end of this chapter outlines the following stages of addiction.)

❖ In the first stage, we simply ***deny*** that we are addicted. We suppress the truth about ourselves and deny that there's a problem. We say to ourselves, "I could stop if I wanted to," "I only do it occasionally," and "I don't have a problem with [whatever our addiction involves]."

❖ The second stage is ***delusion,*** and this has been called sincere denial. We genuinely believe that we don't have a problem. Our addiction is right, acceptable, okay. We have altered our ethical and moral standards to justify our actions, and we build our life around the opportunity to indulge in our addiction.

❖ Then we enter the third stage, the ***dishonest*** stage. We protect our secret world with lies about where we've been and how we spend our time and our money. Our addiction becomes the focus of our attention, and we will let that addiction distort our relationships, our use of time, and our budget. This kind of dishonesty is inevitable because our world is such a private one, and this kind of dishonesty comes quite easily because we desperately want to protect our secret.

Our dishonesty at this point will also involve lying to ourselves about who God is, who we are, and what other people think. When we lie about God, our already-lowered morals become relative; we do what seems right for us in a given situation. Once we have ungodly morals, we develop an incorrect theology that, for instance, might claim that God is a God of love who would never punish us.

❖ At the fourth stage of addiction, we experience a more complete ***distortion of reality***. Besides thinking wrongly about God, we also tend to think that other people are thinking as we are. At this point, we don't consider long-range or short-term consequences for our actions.

❖ The fifth stage of addiction involves ***defensiveness***. When someone points out our behavior, we angrily defend our behavior. In our dishonest and secret world, we have been able to justify our actions, and we will do so to anyone who confronts us. We may respond with "It gives me energy," "It helps me sleep," or "Why are you picking on me?"

❖ Finally, we reach a point of ***despair***. We may find ourselves wanting to give up even trying to change because of our deep sense of shame and guilt. We may vow that we will never again indulge in our addiction, but when we fail, our despair is even more profound. We may even consider suicide at this point when we are asking ourselves, "Why even try? I can't change." Unfortunately, rather than leading to freedom, this despair leads us further into our addiction as we medicate the pain of our shame and guilt with our addiction.

## Freedom from Addiction

Some people think that to control an addiction, one must simply control the addict's behavior, but restoration is not merely behavior modification. Restoration is an inward change in the negative attitudes (doubt, guilt, fear, sadness, separation) rooted in unmet childhood needs that we sought to have met through our addictions. When these and other painful emotions are not dealt with, they can lead to addictions. And an addiction cannot be controlled, a fact which addicts must admit. We must confess our powerlessness over our addiction and trust the power of God to set us free.

To deal with the addiction we must deal with more than the act. We must also experience an internal change, and that change will take time. Just as a person does not become an addict overnight, neither does an addict quickly become free.

## Escaping the Power of Addictions

My efforts to escape my sexual addiction reveal the power an addiction can have. When I first began dealing with my sexual addiction, I began putting on weight until I had gained over thirty pounds. I was exchanging one addiction for another. Now, instead of taking care of my emotional needs through sex, I was feeding my feelings by overeating.

Besides exchanging one addiction for another, I realized that I—like many other people—had to deal with several addictions at one time. I found, for instance, that my ministry was addictive and that being busy was an addiction (I had to be busy reading or doing something all the time). When I was struggling to be free of my sexual addiction, I had to address these other addictions as well.

Sadly, an addiction will have serious consequences not only for our life but also for the lives of people around us. Part of the tragedy of addiction is that it affects other people as well as the addict. In fact, unless we turn to God and receive His gracious help, our addiction can go on to affect generations of people. But admitting our powerlessness over our addictions and trusting in the power of God is the first step toward freedom from our addictions, however many we are struggling with and however long we have been relying on them to meet our needs.

### *Your Own Story*

- *Who has been a Sharon in your life? Who has spoken words of tough love to you to help you, for instance, see the truth about yourself and move towards freedom and healing?*
- *Where (if at all) did you see yourself in the list of Dr. May's five characteristics of addiction? If his list was a mirror for you, what are you going to do about the reflection you saw?*
- *Whether you are struggling with an addiction in your life or with a persistent pattern of sin, confess to God your powerlessness over it. Ask Him to be with you when the temptation is greatest and you are weakest, and ask Him to help you trust Him more for healing and help.*

## Identifying an Addiction

**The Need for More**

We continually need the feeling that the addiction originally provided.

**Withdrawal Symptoms or Symptoms of Stress**

We feel anxious or stressed when opportunities for the addictive experience are limited or unavailable.

**Deception**

We falsely believe that the need for the high is not a problem and that we can discontinue our activity at any time.

**A Loss of Willpower**

We can't say no to the activity.

**Distortion of Attention**

Meeting the addiction becomes the most important thing in life.

*Based on **Addiction and Grace** by Dr. Gerald May*

## Stages of Addiction

| | |
|---|---|
| Denial: | "I could stop if I wanted to." "I only do it occasionally." "I don't have a problem." |
| Delusion: | We change our ethical and moral standards to justify our actions. We build our life around the opportunity to meet our addiction needs. |
| Dishonesty: | We protect our secret world with lies about money, trips, our work schedule, our whereabouts, etc. |
| Distortion of Reality: | We don't consider either the long-range or short-term consequences of our actions. We believe that others think the same way that we do. |
| Defensiveness: | We become angry when we're confronted about our activity. We justify our actions: "It gives me energy"; "It helps me sleep." |
| Despair: | Feeling hopeless and ashamed, we vow never to indulge in our addiction again. We may consider suicide. |

In our despair, we turn to our addiction to medicate the pain.

CHAPTER ❦ SEVEN

# The Mystery of Iniquity

*Why had I, as a four- and five-year-old child, been so bothered by an unnatural sexual curiosity? As I shared my confusion with a friend, I said that it was as though I had been hooked into some unseen influence I couldn't explain.*

As we continue trying to fill our unmet needs with our systems of addiction, we hurt not only ourselves but the people around us. In fact, living according to these systems which are contrary to the will of God will inevitably affect our children and our children's children—and this pattern dates back to Old Testament times. Thousands of years ago, one generation's sins affected the lives of succeeding generations just as our sins today affect our children and our grandchildren (Lev. 26). Even in Moses' day when God issued the commandment forbidding idolatry, He said, "For I, the LORD your God, am a jealous God, visiting the iniquity of the fathers on the children, on the third and the fourth generations of those who hate Me" (Ex. 20:5). When we choose to follow an idol rather than the Lord, God promises to visit our iniquity upon our children, our grandchildren, and our great-grandchildren. And we are choosing an idol over the Lord when we make our addiction the focus of our life.

## The Iniquity of Our Fathers

In *The Sexual Addiction,* Dr. Patrick Carnes writes that all addictions are multiple and generational. In introducing his book, he says, "For the addict, part of therapy is to discover the role of the previous generation in the addiction. The exhibitionist who learned that his father, two uncles, and two cousins were also exhibitionists becomes keenly aware of how the sins of one generation are visited upon the next. Yet for years he was convinced that he was the only one afflicted with the compulsion, a myth which added to the shame and pain at the core of his addiction. The sins and iniquity of his father were indeed visited on him. Many addicts find that the patterns of compulsion are learned quite early in the form of abuse, seduction, or simply witnessing compulsiveness in others" (p. viii).

Abuse is an obvious example of the sins of the father affecting his children, but the effects of a father's sins can visit succeeding generations in many more subtle but no less damaging ways. At this point, however, I want to make a distinction between sin and iniquity.

❖ A sin is an act that violates the will of God.

❖ Iniquity, however, is ongoing. Coming from the Hebrew *avown* and meaning "bentness toward," iniquity points to a lifestyle of sin, to a lawless system of behavior, or, in our terms, an addiction through which we act out unmet needs from the past. As a system of behavior, iniquity seems to possess a life of its own ("the body of this death" [Rom. 7:24], the "body of sin" [Rom. 6:6], "former manner of life" and "the old self" [Eph. 4:22]). In Romans 1, we see that, generation after generation, the Gentiles did not honor God, and that ongoing lawlessness is—to use a phrase from the Bible—"the mystery of iniquity" at work (2 Thess. 2:7 KJV). And we may be able to see the mystery of iniquity at work in our own family's history.

## Roots of Iniquity

Patterns of iniquity develop in much the same way that our systems of addiction develop, and 2 Thessalonians 2:7-11 offers an overview (also, see the chart at the end of this chapter). The seed of iniquity is failure to "receive the love of the truth so as to be saved" (2 Thess. 2:10), the same failure that we found behind our addictions. People suppress the truth that human beings are created in God's image, in His likeness, and to share in His dominion. When the needs which would allow us to experience the sense of self, the sense of order, and the sense of purpose that we are designed to experience are not met, the results are bitterness, anger, the fear of further loss, and unbelief.

These unmet needs and the consequent emotions are "a deluding influence so that they might believe what is false" (2 Thess. 2:11), and this influence leads to the establishment of a false belief system. When we don't receive God's truth, we will believe what is false. We begin to believe, for instance, that we must be our own god because God can't or won't meet our deepest longings. We begin to believe that there are no consequences for our behavior. We then devise our own false way of living, and living out these systems results in a life of sin, transgression, guilt, shame, and fear. Looking to something or someone other than God to be our life source and meet our needs, we find ourselves living an idolatrous life and taking "pleasure in wickedness" (2 Thess. 2:12). And our godless, idolatrous life affects the people around us.

Our acts of iniquity—our systems and addictions—are grounded in our own unmet needs, and that fact is key to understanding why our actions affect the people around us. When we are broken and hurting, we can not give to others—perhaps most especially our spouse and our children—what they need from us. Because we can not adequately fulfill our obligations to them, those people whom we are to care for will end up with unmet needs. We who have an addiction will be so concerned about meeting our needs with our addiction that we will not be aware of or concerned about our children's needs. Unless God intervenes, our parenting—our lifestyle of iniquity—will harm our children and, by creating more people with unmet childhood needs, our children's children.

## The Mystery of Lawlessness

Despite our insight into how parents with unmet needs raise children with unmet needs who grow up to be adults with unmet needs, the working of iniquity remains something of a mystery. And *mystery* implies that which can only be understood with the aid of the Holy Spirit. On our own, without divine revelation, we can not completely understand the nature of iniquity and its ability to exert its influence through the generations.

The generational influences of iniquity may sometimes be hard to prove, but the patterns are there. And those patterns suggest that lawlessness or iniquity seems to be transmitted primarily through unhealthy family systems and negative values, through the environment (society and its secular values, for instance), and through the demonization of a family system. An unnatural sexual curiosity in a four-year-old may be the result of activities he's witnessed at home, comments he's heard (whether or not they were directed specifically to him), the ideas of his playmates, a movie or television program he stumbled upon, his father's inappropriate behavior towards his mother—and Satan can use any or all these types of things to steer us away from God and His will for our life.

One day after I explained the mystery of iniquity, an irate father came up to me. I had made the statement that there is no such thing as a secret affair or activity because it may be lived out in our children and the people we're responsible for. All too often children start manifesting through their behavior the feelings of their parents. But this man didn't agree. He said that the idea that the sins of the fathers could affect their children was an Old Testament concept no longer relevant in the twentieth century. I referred him to 1 Peter 1:18-19 which says, "Knowing that you were not redeemed with perishable things like silver or gold from your futile way of life inherited from your forefathers, but with precious blood, as of a lamb unblemished and spotless, the blood of Christ." The New Testament as well as the Old refers to "a futile way of life" being inherited from our parents, and the realities of the twentieth century confirm the mystery of iniquity and its passage from one generation to the next.

## An Old Testament Example

The prophet Isaiah offers an Old Testament example of iniquity which can help us better understand the mystery of lawlessness, but we first need some New Testament wisdom as background. In Ephesians, Paul teaches that "our struggle is not against flesh and blood, but against the rulers, against the powers, against the world forces of this darkness, against the spiritual forces of wickedness in the heavenly places" (6:12). Behind physical rebellion against God, Paul is saying, lies a spiritual force. Often an evil nation is led by an evil person who is influenced by an evil power. And Isaiah's prophecies about the king of Babylon will show us the evil spiritual power of Satan that is behind the king.

In chapter 14, Isaiah writes, "How you have fallen from heaven, O star of the morning, son of the dawn! You have been cut down to the earth, you who have weakened the nations!" (v. 12). His prophecy against the king of Babylon also refers to the fall of Satan from heaven, and much is revealed about the character of Satan in his five "I will" statements. These statements (Isa. 14:13-14) reveal the demonic power of iniquity and the overarching desire to maintain the self. A chart at the end of this chapter shows how our human drives correspond to these five statements:

- "I will ascend to heaven" indicates self-righteousness rather than righteousness through the blood of Jesus Christ. Self-righteousness seeks to be known for its own good works. In a system like this, approval is thought to be given based on performance.

- "I will raise my throne above the stars of God" is a statement of arrogant self-exaltation and indicates a system designed to bring glory and honor to the self.

❖ "I will sit on the mount of assembly in the recesses of the north" is a prideful pronouncement of self-appointment. Such self-promotion, based on a high opinion of oneself, is fueled by a drive to belong.

❖ "I will ascend above the heights of the clouds" reveals a desire for self-display and a striving to be recognized for one's talents and achievements.

❖ "I will make myself like the Most High" suggests the desire to be self-sustaining. This goal of self-sufficiency, which includes an element of self-preservation, reflects the desire to be looked up to as better than others and the drive to be independent. Depending on others is seen as being controlled by them.

With these five "I will" iniquity drives of Satan in mind, consider the description of "the man of lawlessness" Paul says is coming: "the son of destruction, who opposes and exalts himself above every so-called god or object of worship, so that he takes his seat in the temple of God, displaying himself as being God" (2 Thess. 2:3-4). Like Satan above, this man opposes the way of God and salvation, exalts himself, takes his seat in God's temple, glories in self-display, seeks to preserve himself, and displays himself as God. Like Satan, this man of sin lives according to the principles of lawlessness which are in sharp contrast to the "I am" character of God and, let me mention, the "Thy will" attitude of Jesus.

## Being vs. Doing

When God introduced Himself in the Old Testament, He said, "I AM THAT I AM" (Ex. 3:14 KJV). God's character is based upon His being, not His doing. His actions are based in His unchanging and holy character, and for that reason He can be trusted. It is in God's nature to do what is true to His character. He may change His ways of dealing with us based on our response to Him, but He Himself never changes.

Satan, however, is a willful creature. His actions are governed by his selfish ambition, and they vary according to the situation. He is unpredictable, doing exactly what he pleases and anything it takes to fulfill an "I will" goal of his. While God's good actions are based in His being, Satan's iniquity is based in his action—and so is our iniquity. How often I have heard people say, "I just need to find out who I am, so I'm going to leave my spouse and my children." Iniquity comes alive with our action.

And often even the actions of us believers reflect iniquity rather than holiness. The apostle Paul knew this struggle. When he writes in Romans 7 about doing the very things that he hated, he is describing the mystery of iniquity. Paul knew that when we enter into fellowship with Jesus, confessing our sins and accepting Him as Lord and Savior, our long-time behaviors and old ways of coping with the challenges of life (including how to get our needs met) do not simply vaporize. Paul knew that what we have learned and experienced in life also does not disappear. The information, data, and systems from the past are still a part of us, and those actions and thoughts independent of God and the character of Jesus Christ still influence how we live.

Like Paul, when we enter the Christian life, we drag our old systems with us. That is why, as I've mentioned before, we are commanded to leave behind our old manner of living and to take off the old self (Eph. 4:22). We are to put an end to that lifestyle which does not reflect our newness in Christ because it is in that former lifestyle that iniquity is still at work even though we are believers. We have only to look at church conflicts, petty or significant, to see that iniquity continues to work in followers of Christ. Those "I will" drives by which we attempt to promote our own needs are drives of iniquity.

## Breaking the Generational Link

Although iniquity can be very powerful, its grip is not invincible. We are not sentenced to live at the mercy of the generational influences of our forefathers' iniquity. In the Psalms, King David suggests how we can break the pattern of generational iniquity and loose the grip of a lifestyle that harms everyone around us at the same time that it harms us. In Psalm 139 we read, "Search me, O God, and know my heart; Try me and know my anxious thoughts; And see if there be any hurtful way in me, and lead me in the everlasting way" (vv. 23-24).

Here, David cries to God to "search me" and "try me." When the Holy Spirit searches us, He brings to light the ways of iniquity we need to leave behind. If, at the prompting of the Holy Spirit's conviction, we confess our iniquity, God is faithful and just to forgive us from all unrighteousness (1 John 1:9). But when we are insensitive to the powerful searching ministry of the Holy Spirit, God tries or tests us. God may, for instance, allow us to be in certain circumstances so that He may reveal to us our own iniquity. He does not do this to destroy; He does this to reveal the drives toward iniquity within us and so bring us to salvation.

The tests come in the form of circumstances which pressure and stretch us, and we experience the "travail" and pains of childbirth as we become Christlike (Gal. 4:19). The travail is a sign that the character of Christ is being birthed in us and that our iniquity is being borne away.

## The Travail of Peter

After my own painful exposure, someone asked me, "Why would God push His own child off a cliff?" I replied that God didn't do that with me and that He doesn't do that to any of His children. What God had actually done, I explained, was to pull me out of the fire of my addiction. And I thought about impetuous Peter whom Jesus knew so well.

In Luke 22, Jesus tells Peter, "Satan has demanded permission to sift you like wheat; but I have prayed for you, that your faith may not fail; and you, when once you have turned again, strengthen your brothers" (31-32). Peter confidently responds, "Lord, with You I am ready to go both to prison and to death!" (22:33).

Jesus knows otherwise and tells Peter that before the cock crows he will have denied Him three times. The Lord recognized in Peter's heart seeds of iniquity, the seeds of self-exaltation and self-righteousness. A degree of glory would come to Peter with a prison sentence or a noble death for Jesus' sake, and Peter's proclamation of faithfulness to Christ until death sounds forth a self-righteous attitude. So Jesus gave permission for the Enemy to bring pressure upon Peter. As the Lord did with Peter, He allows our own transgressions to surface so that we will come to Him. He does not do this in judgment. He does this in mercy so that we will draw closer to Him.

It is strange and curious that Christ allows what is in the heart to be revealed. When Peter saw his weakness for what it was, he learned he would need to rely on the strength of the Lord rather than his own power. The Lord allowed Peter's weakness to surface so that he would become the person God wanted him to become. This kind of divine set-up exposes the sin that is in our hearts, invites us to confess that sin, and teaches us about the kind of person God wants us to be.

## The Family History

In ministering to a person caught in an addiction, we need to look not just at that individual but at his or her whole family. Almost everyone who has studied addictions has found that generational influences are very evident in an addict's family. I remember the man who came to see me about sexual addiction. Byron was the fourth of five children and, as we looked at his family history, he remembered that his father was an alcoholic involved in sexual addiction. Byron also knew that his grandfather had died an alcoholic. When I asked about his mother, Byron said that she never interfered with her husband's interest in pornography. He also said that, while she was growing up, her older brother had molested her and later her younger brother became an alcoholic.

With this overview of his family tree, I was able to share with Byron that his mother had cooperated with his father's addiction simply by not doing anything, by being nonconfrontive. When she was molested, her boundaries had been removed, and later she didn't know when or how to draw limits of protection for herself or anyone else. She didn't know when she could or couldn't make a request, how to confront, or when it was appropriate. Consequently, she enabled her husband's addiction. As Byron realized how family systems influenced his life, he was able to see his life for what it was and eventually overcome his addiction.

When we look at family systems in the same way Byron and I looked at his family, we bring iniquities to light. Sometimes that action—the mere exposure of iniquity—dissolves the power of the iniquity and frees us from its hold. Other times, bringing the iniquity of the family to light helps us see how to dismantle the system that traps us, and, by the grace of God, we can begin to change patterns of iniquity passed down through the generations.

## Travail: God at Work

We who have claimed salvation and experienced new birth in Jesus Christ may continue to feel influences on our life from earlier generations. Asking God to search us and then responding with true repentance to the conviction of the Holy Spirit may help us to escape the power of the past. Sometimes, however, the path to freedom will involve being tried and tested and experiencing the travail—the pressuring and stretching—of new birth. It is by travail that Christ is formed in us just as it was by travail that Jesus submitted Himself to God as the perfect sacrifice for our sins (Rom. 4:25, Isa. 53:11).

In the book of Acts, we see how God birthed life in the early church by pressuring and stretching His people. Pressures of theological differences, for example, led to revival and an open door to the Gentile world. Pressures of drought and financial need united the Jewish and the Gentile believer. When the church was failing in its missionary endeavors, God allowed persecution which resulted in a prayer ministry and a heart for missions. As the church experienced the pressures of growth and expansion, church order and ministries were established. When the widows were being neglected, the church began to select deacons, an example of God bringing forth order when there was the pressure of unmet needs. In the early church and in the life of modern-day believers, God uses pressure and stretching to birth that which He desires in His people. As believers, we should not be surprised if we experience pressure in our lives until Christ is formed in us.

## Standing Strong

In Isaiah 53 we are told that Jesus bore our sorrows, "was pierced through for our transgressions . . . [and] was crushed for our iniquities" (4-5). When we experience the pressure of the mystery of iniquity still present in our life and the stretching and travail of Jesus being born in us, we need to more fully appropriate the power of this gospel message. We need to more fully receive all that Jesus has done for us on the cross.

❖ We can stand in the providence of the Cross. In Galatians 3:13-14 we read, "Christ redeemed us from the curse of the Law, having become a curse for us—for it is written, 'Cursed is everyone who hangs on a tree'—in order that in Christ Jesus the blessing of Abraham might come to the Gentiles, so that we might receive the promise of the Spirit through faith." It is not God's plan that we should continue in the mystery of iniquity, and that is why He sent Jesus to be made a curse for us. At the Cross we can be made free from the power of the past. We must accept this freedom. We are members of the new family of God, and as such we can bring healing to our natural family by breaking the generational link.

❖ We break this generational link by first recognizing its pattern and its influence. Our family can be either a fountain of life or a cesspool out of which all its members drink. When it is a cesspool, we need to recognize that and stop drinking from it because the poison will kill. In order to understand the power behind our addictions, we must understand what iniquity is and acknowledge how the sins of our fathers contributed to our addiction.

❖ Once we gain this insight, we then need to work on taking off our old self and discarding our old systems. We need to put on Jesus

Christ. We need to allow Him who dwells in us to flow outward from us through our actions. We need to live out our faith in behaviors that honor God and meet our needs in a healthy way.

Generational influences will continue to have a hold on us until they are broken by the grace of God. And the grace of God will give us the hope and the strength we need to let go of our systems of addictions, to face our hurts, and to find restoration in Him.

## Your Own Story

- *Where do you see yourself in the "I will" statements? Are the seeds of iniquity apparent in your attitudes or goals for yourself? Let God's Holy Spirit search you.*
- *When has God allowed circumstances to bring you to the point of recognizing your iniquity? Be specific about what God showed you, how He showed you, and what you learned. Now consider whether God may be using current circumstances to help you acknowledge sin in your life. Spend a few minutes prayerfully considering this possibility.*
- *What behavior patterns—bad habits or even addictions—do you see in your family history? What actions, thought patterns, ways of interacting, or methods of dealing with problems do you see in your grandparents, your parents, and yourself? Acknowledge these patterns and, in prayer, claim the power of the Cross to help you overcome them.*

## The Development of Iniquity

*2 Thessalonians 2:10-12*

*"They did not receive the love of the truth . . ."*

When we rejected God's image, God's likeness, and God's dominion as the design for our life, we are rejecting God's love as well as the opportunity to be a channel of His love to others.

*"They believed what is false . . ."*

Our rejection of God's design was the result of our unbelief. Not believing God, we didn't follow His plan for us. We devised our own false way to meet our needs and live our life.

*"They took pleasure in wickedness . . ."*

Our false way included a choice that would be pleasurable.

## The "I Will" Statements of Satan and the Iniquity Drives of Human Beings

*Isaiah 14:13-14*

| | |
|---|---|
| Self-Righteousness: | "I will ascend to heaven." |
| Self-Exaltation: | "I will raise my throne above the stars of God." |
| Self-Appointment: | "I will sit on the mount of assembly in the recesses of the north." |
| Self-Display: | "I will ascend above the heights of the clouds." |
| Self-Sustaining: | "I will make myself like the Most High." |

Note how our human drives correspond to the "I will" statements of Satan.

| | |
|---|---|
| Self-Righteousness: | The human drive to be accepted on the basis of our good works.<br>We feel that approval is based on performance. |
| Self-Exaltation: | We strive to bring honor and glory to self.<br>We want to be looked up to by others. |
| Self-Appointment: | We desire to belong.<br>We will promote ourselves without regard for the ministry and abilities of others. |
| Self-Display: | We seek to be recognized for our personal achievements.<br>We may even want to be idolized. |
| Self-Sustaining: | We want to be independent and self-sufficient.<br>We view being dependent on people as being controlled by them. |

CHAPTER ❦ EIGHT

# Grieving Our Loss

*Slowly and deliberately, I read the letter to the small support group. Each of us had been told to write to the person who was the source of our greatest hurt, and the actual writing had been agonizing. I had waited to be the last one to read, and I could put it off no longer. "Dear Dad," I began, and tears started to flow. I apologized for those tears and fought to hold them back, but the emotions of a lifetime seemed to gush forth. For the first time, I was able to feel the insatiable needs, pain, and denial of the past and to grieve my loss.*

One time during a counseling session with Sharon, I talked about my journey of restoration. After listening to some of my testimony and experience, she said, "Don, you're in a low-grade depression, aren't you?" I didn't know much about low-grade depression, but I did know that I had spent several months eating a lot, sleeping a lot, and trying to block out what had happened to me.

Sharon then explained that I hadn't allowed myself to grieve my loss and suggested that I needed to grieve and even cry. That was a stunning remark. I had learned long before that men don't cry, and my religious training had wrongly taught me that if I grieved my loss, then I really had not repented. This strong resistance to expressing sorrow and crying over loss had led me to turn my feelings of sorrow inward. The result was, in fact, depression.

## What the Bible Teaches

With Sharon's words in mind, I opened the Scripture to see if it was okay for me to grieve my loss—and I was amazed by the various references to grief.

❖ I had heard a television preacher say that it was wrong to cry at the funeral of a loved one. He quoted the Scripture from 1 Thessalonians which says we are not "to grieve like the rest of men, who have no hope" (4:13 NIV). But a careful reading of this verse shows simply that our grief is not to be like the hopeless who don't know the Lord. Paul does not say that we can not grieve.

❖ The passages I studied in Scripture always allowed a time for grief. As I began to read Lamentations—an entire book of sorrow!—I found a series of laments over the destruction of Jerusalem. The first chapter alone was enough to assure me that the sorrow I was experiencing was okay.

❖ In the book of Psalms, I read that David wept and poured out his heart before God. I learned from David that we needn't be ashamed of sorrow, and I saw in the New Testament that sorrow is to be shared (Gal. 6:2).

❖ In Matthew 5:4, Jesus says, "Blessed are those who mourn, for they shall be comforted." Although Jesus doesn't specify the reason for the mourning, He also doesn't say that mourners will be scorned, ridiculed, or shunned. No, those who mourn will be blessed, and this promise from my Savior offered me hope.

❖ In 2 Corinthians 7:10, I read, "For godly sorrow worketh repentance to salvation not to be repented of: but the sorrow of the world worketh death" (KJV). Here, I saw, first, that sorrow could play an important role in bringing about repentance for those actions which caused the sorrow and, second, that repentance—turning to God—would mean experiencing God's grace and love.

## Grieving and Repentance

One day as I was meditating on sorrow, I felt God ask me what godly sorrow was. In the past, I had defined it as anything that breaks the heart of God. I also knew that Scripture speaks of grieving the Holy Spirit.

Then God seemed to ask me if I really believed that my sins had broken His heart. I thought about my resignation from the church and the difficult consequences of that move. At the time of my resignation and now as I remembered those days, I cried over how I had brought such reproach to the cause of Christ and allowed mockery to be made of God's truth and the standards which I had formerly proclaimed. Feeling a great sorrow, I realized that never again did I want to grieve the Holy Spirit or bring reproach upon the kingdom of God. In moments like this, godly sorrow can bring about repentance, a change of behavior, a new approach to life.

Another question came from God. Did I believe that His heart had been broken over my sins against others? At this point, God allowed me to feel the grief and the loneliness my wife had experienced when

I was so often away from home. She knew something was wrong, but she didn't know what it was. She was lonely when I wasn't home at night. And she suffered from the emotional separation we had experienced. I felt an overwhelming sorrow for the pain I had caused Helen. The Holy Spirit allowed me to grieve over my sins against Helen so that I would change my life and not hurt her again. Now I could heal and help make her happy. Now our life together could be one of fulfillment.

Soon after my tears for Helen, I felt the Lord leading me to go to a nearby city, and there I experienced sorrow for the pain I had caused my children. I thought the Lord had led me to the city to meditate on Him. When I got there, I found a small hotel that was very quiet and lonely. Still not sure exactly why I was supposed to be there, I got in my car to find a fast-food restaurant for dinner. As I drove, I found myself heading toward the university my daughter had attended, and I saw in my mind various images of her. Although she had many friends, in my mind I pictured her alone in her little car crying. The Holy Spirit was allowing me to experience some of the hurt my daughter had experienced because of my insensitivity. The Holy Spirit also reminded me that I had only visited her three times in four years and that I hadn't called her while she was there. I saw how negligent I had been because of my addiction. I was sobbing so deeply that I could hardly see to drive. Filled with sorrow and grief, I returned to my room and fell onto the bed. Throughout the night, I felt the hurt that I caused my family.

I had a similar experience with memories of my son. I remembered some times of closeness, but I also remembered the many times of separation and loss. I hadn't provided the nurturing he needed, and so I had hindered the presence of God's glory in his life and the presence of God's glory which He had intended to exist within the family structure. Feeling my own pain was hard enough, but feeling the pain I had caused others—especially my wife and my children—because of my selfishness and sinfulness was almost unbearable.

## Grieving Sins against Us

About two years after I resigned from the church, I was beginning to be released back into ministry by the Christian leaders that I was accountable to. One Sunday morning, some college students from my former church were attending the church where I was speaking. They came up to me after the service and told me that they loved me and that they hadn't lost respect for me or my ministry. Prompted by the

Holy Spirit, I asked their forgiveness, and they readily forgave me.

One young woman, however, said there was something she wanted to share. Saying first that she didn't want to hurt me, she went on to ask me if I understood the hurt that members of the church had experienced because of my sin and my resignation. Others in the community had ridiculed them and made jokes about the situation; it had cost church members to be a part of the fellowship. Over the next several weeks, I grieved for having hurt the members of that church. The Holy Spirit allowed me to experience their pain in a small way.

Grief like this is a hallmark of healing and restoration in our spiritual life. It is when we become well—physically or, in this case, spiritually—that we can begin to see the pain of someone else. As God brings healing to our lives, we can experience the loss that those around us have experienced because of our sin.

Even though I was becoming aware of other people's loss because of my sin, my sorrowing was not yet over. At this point, God asked me if I thought His heart had been broken because of other people's sins against me. I knew that my sins had brought pain to my family, to my friends, and even to God, but I had not considered what I had lost as a result of other people's sins against me. So I began to deal with my grief about my own loss. Unless we grieve over how other people's sins have hurt us and caused us loss, our grieving will not be complete.

## The Consequences of Not Grieving

And that completion or closure to our sorrow is important to a healthy, forward-looking life. Finding closure may mean tracing loss throughout our childhood memories and experiences. The embarrassments during high school, the loss of a pet, the betrayal of friends, the regrets of not working harder—we need to bring closure to these events from the past even if the adult voice inside is downplaying their significance. Until we can release the sorrow of the world and release the anger against those who have hurt us, we may face devastating emotional, physical, and spiritual consequences.

One such consequence, we're warned in Hebrews, is the appearance of the "root of bitterness" (12:15). Bitterness takes hold when we are not able to forgive ourselves or those involved in the painful circumstances we've experienced. God can enable us to forgive and so prevent the growth of bitterness which can defile us and the people around us, especially if those people remind us of the ones who have hurt us. Releasing the past can protect us from bitterness.

If bitterness does arise, it can darken our understanding about

God. As I've explained before, that darkened understanding about who God is and who we are to be leads to systems that ensnare (Eph. 4:17-19). When we have not dealt with past hurts or forgiven those people who hurt us, we may live out these unresolved situations and feelings in compulsive addictive behavior or problematic relationships. We will experience a reparative drive to somehow fix that which was never complete in us, be it a sense of self, a sense of belonging, or a sense of purpose.

Also, if we don't deal with the pain and grief of past hurts, we will be unable to fully appreciate the love that was expressed in the past or that is being expressed to us today. Furthermore, childhood losses that we have not dealt with often become the basis for our response to situations in our adult life. If we are to live as emotionally mature adults, we need to have brought closure to our childhood hurts.

Until we forgive ourselves or those involved in the pain of the past or until we release the anger and hurt to the Lord, we will suffer physically as well as emotionally. If we don't complete the grieving process, we can experience stomach ulcers, allergies, heart disease, and a lowered immune system.

We will also experience spiritual problems. If we are stuck in the hurts of childhood, for instance, we may find ourselves dealing with a sense of incompleteness or an inability to mature. Being stuck in unforgiveness also leads us to distrust other people as well as God.

But, with God's grace, we can grieve our loss, forgive those who contributed to the loss, and then move on from the hurts of the past. If, however, we offer forgiveness on a purely intellectual level, we will live *out* our hurt through anger, rage, or rebellion, or we will live *in* our hurt and close down emotionally and isolate ourselves from people. Forgiveness from the heart comes when we have fully grieved, and that grief involves two kinds of sorrow.

## Godly Sorrow and Sorrow of the World

When I turned to the Bible to learn about grieving, I learned that godly sorrow is different from the sorrow of the world (see the charts at the end of this chapter for a comparison as well as a list of major causes of sorrow).

❖ Godly sorrow is a sorrow over the loss of God's glory and the wickedness of sin. Godly sorrow sees from the eternal perspective and so understands something of the spiritual significance of events on earth. In contrast, sorrow of the world is a sorrow over personal loss and the painful consequences of one's sinful actions. Its scope is limited to the physical and the temporal.

❖ Godly sorrow recognizes the loss that we and others experience because of our own sin and shortcomings. Sorrow of the world, however, blames others for our problems and so results in self-pity.

❖ Godly sorrow views circumstances with God's purposes in mind and so works repentance. When we begin to see through the eyes of God's grace, we can see God even in our failures. And, despite our failures, we can receive the redeeming and restorative grace of God at the same time that we acknowledge and address the consequences of our actions. The world's sorrow, though, results in hopelessness and depression because sorrows and difficult circumstances are not seen as part of God's design.

## The Results of Godly Sorrow

Godly sorrow produces repentance and brings freedom. In 2 Corinthians 7:11, Paul tells us more about the results of godly sorrow and godly grief:

❖ Vindication: We will find a new desire to correct our wrong behavior. We will want to establish a new credibility and testimony to God's goodness and His faithfulness to us who are sinners.

❖ Indignation: Having seen the consequences of our sinful behavior, we will feel a new hatred for sin. At the same time, we will have renewed compassion for the sinner.

❖ Godly Fear or Awe: Looking at life from the perspective of eternity, we will be more sensitive to God's presence and His control of the events of our life. Also, fear of the Lord is the beginning of wisdom (Prov. 1:7), and that wisdom will help us become more aware of what causes the loss of God's glory.

❖ Longing: When we sense a loss of God's glory, we will long to fill that vacuum in our soul with His love. Before, we were driven to meet our own needs; now we have a passion for Christ and His glory.

❖ Zeal: A person focused on his or her own emotional needs will often lack energy and enthusiasm for life. It takes energy to be angry, fearful, and bitter. As we become free of that pain, we will find a new level of energy and a new zeal for the things of God.

❖ Justice: We will have developed a new sensitivity to injustice and the power of sin. This sensitivity together with the lessons we learned from our own failure will give us the desire to help others escape the bondage that held us.

## Grieving Godly Sorrow

The grieving process for our godly sorrow involves two steps. First we become aware of what has broken the heart of God (our sins against Him and our sins against others). This awareness means feeling the pain we have caused people and, especially, our heavenly Father. As we feel this pain, we experience to a small degree the pain we have caused God and others.

Acknowledging our sin and feeling something of the pain we caused leads us, by God's grace, to repent for our sin. And genuine repentance involves a change of direction, a change in our lifestyle. Although this two-step process may sound simple, it isn't easy to do. By God's grace, however, we can walk through the process to a new freedom for sin and a new joy in pleasing Him.

## Grieving the Sorrow of the World

God's grace not only helps us experience the pain of godly sorrow and the repentance it brings, but His grace also helps us deal with the sorrow of the world, sorrow for the consequences and personal loss in the here and now. I, for instance, had to grieve the dishonor I had brought upon my family, the financial hardship caused by my resignation and having to live off savings, the loss of friends who didn't know what to do or say, and the loss of friends who pulled away from us. I also felt sorrow for the years of creativity I had wasted (I had spent much creative energy pursuing my addiction) and the health I had lost (the tremendous stress of worry, guilt, and fear took their toll). I also felt a profound grief over the loss of my ministry and my dreams. All of this sorrowing and grieving was part of my restoration process. The sorrowing and grieving helped me let go of the things of the past, the things of our addiction which were an anchor and an idol. But after we feel this sorrow of the world, we must release it, and that happens in several stages (see the chart at the end of this chapter).

### *Stage One: Denial*

I had long dreamed of building a relationship with my father—and then he died. As I conducted the funeral service, I felt anger rather than sadness. For years after his death, I couldn't visit his grave. Whenever we were in the area, Helen suggested that we stop by, but I would not go. I was denying the reality of what was lost: I had lost my father and any chance of building a relationship with him. I denied the significance of the loss I was experiencing.

### *Stage Two: Anger*

At this stage, we feel our loss, and we are angry because we feel we've been violated. We direct our anger toward those whom we judge responsible for our sorrow. If we deny this anger, it can manifest itself in a variety of unhealthy ways. After my father died, for instance, my involvement in the world of sexual addiction intensified as I lived out the anger I felt toward him. My sexual perversion was a search for the love of a father, a love which his death had forever deprived me of. From that point, I medicated whatever pain occurred in my life with my sexual addiction.

### *Stage Three: Depression*

Depression is a feeling of hopelessness that can lead us to God. Depression can help us realize that we can't meet our deepest needs and that only God can. If we don't deal with our depression, though, it will not lead us to God. Instead, depression—which has been defined as anger turned inward—will become self-destructive, and we may find ourselves feeling suicidal.

### *Stage Four: Sadness*

The fourth stage of grieving is sadness, and this stage is important because here we begin to say good-bye to the past and let go of it. In our sadness, we accept our loss, but we do so with a view to the future. We don't deny the past, but we do acknowledge that the past is past. Here we begin to find release. I know that I began to experience release at this point. . . .

Sharon, my counselor, asked me to write a letter to my father to say good-bye. This was not to be a love letter or a letter to dishonor him. I was simply to express my loss and say good-bye. It took me more than a month to write this letter. My pain was too deep and my denial too strong. I found that I couldn't remember—much less feel—all the sorrow for the past, and it is through sorrow that we get in touch with our pain and loss. I appreciated Sharon's suggestion that I begin the letter with "The things which I would like to have received from you while I was growing up and never did were . . ."

Sharon instructed me to write a letter, not just make a list. I was to write in a realistic manner so as to release my pain and come to a point of forgiveness. When I read my letter to Sharon, I was surprised by the tears that welled up inside me. Occasionally, she would affirm my hurt, cringing with me and acknowledging that a certain statement or action must have indeed been hurtful. With that modeling, I came to understand in a new way that Jesus, the high priest, could feel our weaknesses (Heb. 4:14-16). Sharon had such a priestly ministry to me as she helped me bear my burdens so that I could in turn release them to Christ. During this period of sadness, it was important that someone affirm my sorrow as Sharon did.

The letter I wrote released me enough from the past that I could move toward genuine forgiveness. I was able to release the past to God who promises to work all things out for the good of them that love Him and are called according to His purposes (Rom. 8:28). Still, it was seven years before I could visit my father's grave and forgive him—and I mean genuine heartfelt forgiveness, not mere verbal forgiveness. Before God and other people, I confessed that I forgave my dad, and I released him from my bitter judgments and unrealistic expectations.

My emotions were fragile and tender for a few weeks, but in time, I went to his grave and I said good-bye to the past. The Holy Spirit reminded me of the hours that my father had labored and worked to take care of his family, and I was able to thank God for my father. Having let go of my sadness, I could focus on good memories of him. By releasing the past, I could also release my father from my expectations that were unfulfilled. I could now trust God to re-father me and minister to the needs that had never been met in my life.

*Stage Five: Forgiveness*

At this point of the grieving process, we experience God's grace and so release others from our bitter judgments. But, as everyone knows, forgiveness doesn't always come easily. When it comes, it often happens in three stages, as the parable of the steward in Matthew 18 illustrates. The steward was ready to have the slave who was in debt, his wife, and his children sold in order to collect the money due. But when the slave fell down, cried for mercy, and promised to repay his debt, the steward "felt compassion and released him and forgave him the debt" (v. 27).

Like the steward, we must first develop a sense of compassion for those who have hurt us. Just as the steward saw the slave as God saw him, we need to see those who hurt us through God's eyes. We need to feel their pain and be touched by those circumstances which led them to act against us. This perspective will then enable us to release them from our bitter judgments about their actions. Finally, we can forgive them the debt: we can release them from the unfulfilled expectations we had for them which they never met. Feel compassion, release, and forgive—these are the three steps of genuine forgiveness, and these three steps are based on God's sovereignty. Let me explain.

We can't forgive without faith in God—without faith in the fact that God is just and merciful; without faith that God is able to take human errors and plans intended to destroy and work them out for His glory and our benefit. (The Old Testament story of Joseph in Genesis 37-50 is an excellent example of God doing just this. When Joseph's brothers sold him into slavery, little did they know that years later his position in Egypt would enable them to survive a great famine.) We can be unforgiving, hold on to the past, and nurse our feelings of self-pity and bitterness and anger toward God. Or we can ask for God's grace to forgive those who have hurt us, and then we can exchange our sense of loss for the peace that comes with knowing God is in control of our life. (See Chapter Twelve for more on forgiveness.)

### *Stage Six: Gratitude*

In the book of Romans, we read, "We know that God causes all things to work together for good to those who love God, to those who are called according to His purpose" (8:28). Notice that the verse does not say that God causes everything. We must acknowledge that Satan works to sabotage God's plan for people's lives. But, claiming the promise from Romans, I was finally able to express my gratitude not for what happened, but for that fact that our sovereign God is able to work out the pain and hurt of the past for His glory and our benefit. I could thank my heavenly Father for using the isolation I had experienced to build a more intimate relationship with Him. I could thank God for using whatever I had lost to make me more sensitive to others. And this kind of gratitude is key to continuing along the path of forgiveness.

During this stage of grieving, I also noticed that many of the negative emotions I had been dealing with were gradually being transformed into the image of Jesus Christ. I could see how my unbelief was being transformed into faith, fear into wisdom, guilt into compassion, and shame into transparency. And the list kept going! I could see sadness being transformed into hope and joy, loneliness into fullness and hope, anger into boldness for God's kingdom, and the sense of separateness and isolation into a deep love and concern for other people. When we—with gratitude toward God—embrace our weaknesses and failures as opportunities for growth and for knowing Him better, we can begin to fully release the past. We may not always feel thankful, but we can continue to give thanks to God.

*Stage Seven: Serenity and Peace*

Having acknowledged our losses and felt sad about them, having forgiven those we needed to forgive, and having thanked God for His sovereignty over even the hurts of our life, we then experience serenity and peace. We experience that peace that passes understanding (Phil. 4:7), and we rest in the knowledge that God is in control of every situation in our life—past, present, and future.

Because sorrow can and does resurface, we may need to go through this grieving process several times, perhaps focusing on a different source of sorrow each time. The surfacing of memories, for instance, may prompt another cycle of grieving. We may remember scenes from our growing-up years, names we were called, times we were overpowered by a sibling, or being the child who got the leftovers or who was left out of a special event. We may also remember details about emotional, physical, or sexual abuse. The grieving process will help us cope with these memories in the same way that it initially helped us let go of the past.

## The Little Boy Inside

In my own grieving process, I had to deal with memories of the past and things lost during my childhood years. And dealing with those memories was just as painful as standing next to my father's grave, saying good-bye, and realizing that he was no longer there to meet my needs. I had come to understand that he, too, was human and that he had experienced his own loss and pain. Even though events during his life journey had kept him from being the father I needed and wanted, saying good-bye still brought about fear and uncertainty. I felt just like a child about to leave home.

In Genesis it is recorded, "For this cause a man shall leave his father and his mother, and shall cleave to his wife; and they shall become one flesh" (2:24). This act of leaving does not mean breaking off communication with our parents or the end of our respect for them. Instead, this verse teaches the importance of emotional separation, a lesson many fail to learn. If the emotional tie to our parents is not broken, we set ourselves up to meet our needs in unhealthy ways. We may marry someone to father or mother us, or we may look to someone in our work place or neighborhood to parent us. We will live according to the lie that someone else will make us happy or that someone else will come by and fix us.

It is painful and frightening, but we need to recognize that the emotional umbilical cord to our parents must be broken. We must give up our expectation that someone will take care of us. We need to sever the emotional tie and recognize that we are responsible for our own happiness and for our relationships with others. When I stood at my father's grave, I was finally able to loosen these emotional ties of the child within. I could now mature in Jesus Christ; I could and must embrace God the Father, for He was now my Father.

When I was driving along not long after that gravesite visit, I suddenly found myself blinded by tears, and I had to pull over to the side of the road. I could clearly see myself as a small child, and I had a strong sense of that little boy's feelings—that little boy whom I had hidden inside of me, whom I had been so ashamed of, and whom I had abandoned in the world of my secret life. That day, however, I embraced that little boy and his emotions. I hugged that part of me that had never grown up. And as I hugged that little boy, so did God the Father. He was there to re-parent that little boy and bring him into adulthood.

After this experience, I sometimes woke up in the middle of the night feeling very lonely. Now, instead of turning to my past addictions to cope with these feelings, I was able to respond to the grace of God. My heavenly Father was there to meet my needs and ease my longings. I no longer had to feel ashamed when I needed closeness or comfort. God the Father was there. And God ministered to me through my wife and my friends as well. I no longer had to look to my past addictions. I had said good-bye to my father, and I was not nursing any fantasies about childhood needs being met. The painful process of sorrow and grief had done its good work.

## The Loss of Our System

Besides grieving for the pain we have caused God, our family, and our friends and colleagues and for the loss we have experienced because of people's sins against us, we may also grieve over the loss of the system we had used to meet our needs. That may sound odd, and I know I was surprised that, after getting free of my sexual addictions and leaving my church, there was still within me a desire to return to my former system of seduction and deception. I noticed, for instance, that when I was trying to help others, I still felt the pull to become more emotionally involved and more of a caretaker than the situation demanded.

Two people—one a counselor and the other a friend—gently but firmly confronted me about letting myself become too emotionally involved. They saw that I could easily allow an emotional dependency to develop, and I knew they were right when, while I was ministering to another person, I thought, "This was how my addiction felt!" That feeling that someone needed me was almost like a drug that offered me a high. When my counselor asked what I was going to do about this emotional addiction that was resurfacing, I knew that I had to reposition the relationship, refer the person I had been meeting with to a professional counselor, and refocus my emotions and passions. I also realized that there was still work to be done on my road to restoration.

Specifically, I needed to say good-bye to addictive behavior and to those systems which had been my companions for a long time. Although the systems brought a sense of pleasure, there was a falsehood in those systems. They suggested that they could meet my needs, but I had learned that systems of addiction can't. Only God our Father can. Still, I wept over letting go of my systems. At first, I didn't understand why there was this great sorrow and grieving. But I soon realized that my systems represented familiar territory for me when it came to having my needs met. I experienced a sense of sorrow and loss as I moved away from this comfort zone. But as I moved away, God was there for me, and I received the grace He extends to all of us.

## Dealing with Sorrow and Pain

Even after we've walked through the grieving process, pain and sorrow can resurface with a new sorrow or the memory of an old sadness. We also need to learn to deal with the kind of sorrow and grief that comes in day-to-day life so that we don't medicate the feelings with our previous addiction. I would like to share four steps that I have found useful in dealing with sorrow and pain.

❖ Recognize Your Sorrow: Don't deny the sorrow or hurt. Don't try to shove the feelings aside. Instead, recognize them in your heart and before God. Let the pain and sorrow you've hidden be brought into the light. When they reach the light, you can begin to see the falsehood of medicating the pain with your addiction instead of trusting God to use the circumstances of sorrow for His glory and your benefit.

❖ Catch Your Sorrow: Once you recognize the sorrow, catch it! Paul tells us to take "every thought captive to the obedience of Christ" (2 Cor. 10:5). Through prayer and meditation on God's Word, we can ask God about His perspective on our pain and His plans for redeeming it. When we take our sorrow to God, we won't find ourselves believing Satan's lies about what will happen next or responding out of our fear and emotions. Grounding ourselves in God's truth will also keep us from building fortresses so that we won't be hurt again. When we shine the spotlight of Christ on our sorrow, He will remind us of His faithfulness. We will find ourselves free to trust God instead of letting our emotions be our god.

❖ Share Your Sorrow: Taking our sorrow captive is an internal step that precedes pouring out our heart to the Lord and, when appropriate, to other people. Like David in the Psalms, we are to share our pain and sorrow. In times of persecution, despair, sorrow, and failure, David cried out to the Lord and trusted in His righteousness and judgment. Christ already knows our anger and our hurt, so we can freely pour out those feelings to Him.

❖ Replace Your Sorrow: When we don't see our loss and sorrow through our Redeemer God's eyes, we can become bitter and focus on the wrongs and weaknesses of others. But when we share our sorrows, hurts, and fears with the Lord, we are able to see our loss made up by His glory. We see that perfect love casts out fear (1 John 4:18). God's love can replace our sorrow, our hurt, and our fear if we open ourselves to receive it.

Loss. We may no longer feel that we are in the presence of the Lord. We may find our relationships with other people strained or broken. We may question our purpose in life. Whatever the cause of our sense of loss, we can turn to God with the sorrow and pain we feel. We can ask Him to walk with us through the grieving process, and we can trust Him to meet our needs for identity, relationship, and purpose. Our heavenly Father will enable us to once again experience His presence where we will find "fulness of joy" (Psalm 16:11); He will bless us with fellowship in His body of believers, another source of joy (1 John 1:3-4); and He will make clear His purpose for us in His kingdom, again so that our joy may be full (John 15:1-11). Our gracious and sovereign God will replace our spirit of heaviness with a garment of praise and our sorrows with a heartfelt joy in Him.

## *Your Own Story*

- ❦ *Perhaps in your life right now there is room for godly sorrow. What have you done that has broken the heart of God? Ask the Holy Spirit to show you where you have hurt God, your family members, or your friends and to guide you to repentance.*
- ❦ *What sins against you might have broken the heart of God? Which of these actions or words do you need to grieve and, in the process, forgive? Again, ask the Holy Spirit to walk through the seven-step process with you.*
- ❦ *Explain in your own words the relationship between forgiveness and faith in God. What encouragement do you find here?*

## Godly Sorrow vs. The Sorrow of the World

| Godly Sorrow | The Sorrow of the World |
|---|---|
| • A sorrow over the loss of God's glory | • A sorrow over personal loss only |
| • Loss of God's glory in others | • Resentment or blaming others for your loss |
| • Personal loss of God's glory | • Self-pity |
| • Circumstances viewed with God's sovereign grace and divine purposes in mind | • Circumstances viewed without a sense of God's sovereign grace or divine purposes |

## Three Major Causes of Sorrow

**Loss of Well-Being, God's Image**

Physical rejection
Abandonment
Childhood trauma
Childhood abuse
Comparing oneself to others
A loss of childhood

**Loss of Relationships, God's Likeness**

Parents (death, divorce, separation)
Friends (moved away, betrayal, death, etc.)
Spouse (divorce, death, estrangement)
Church division
God (unanswered prayers, guilt, disbelief, etc.)

**Loss of Purpose, God's Dominion**

Job loss
Passed over for promotion
Stuck in career
Financial loss
Loss of health (disease, injury, aging)

## The Grieving Process

| | |
|---|---|
| **Denial:** | Fear and shock may cause loss of memory.<br>We may try to justify what happened rather than feel the pain.<br>We may bargain with God rather than deal with the reality. |
| **Anger:** | We feel the hurt.<br>We direct our angry feelings toward those we judge responsible. |
| **Depression:** | This hopelessness is healthy if it leads us to depend on God.<br>This can be unhealthy if we don't deal with it and continue in a downward emotional spiral. |
| **Sadness:** | Here we begin to start letting go.<br>This feeling helps us say good-bye to the past. |
| **Forgiveness:** | We release others from our bitter judgments.<br>We trust God to use our past hurts for His glory and our benefit. |
| **Embrace:** | We embrace our weaknesses and care for the child within.<br>We are able to thank God for turning our failures into opportunities for growth. |
| **Serenity and Peace:** | We rest in the knowledge that God is in control of our life—the past, the present, and the future. |

CHAPTER ❦ NINE

# Embracing Our Weakness

*I could look at that old photograph of myself as a child for a long time. I would see the sandy-blond hair and the twinkle in his eyes, but I would also see his deep sadness. Something about him—about me—seemed to cry out, "Somebody please help me!" And how often I wanted to do just that. I wanted to reach into the picture—into his loneliness, fear, and pain—and hold the little boy close to me. I wanted to ease his pain, speak words of truth about his value, and offer him the kind of love he didn't feel.*

Through grieving and forgiveness, we release the pains and hurts of the past, and we need to do so. If we don't, we will continually try to repair the past; we will keep trying to cover the pain through compulsive and addictive behavior. (A wise friend commented that the more we try to make a successful yesterday, the less we will be able to make a hopeful tomorrow!) Releasing the pain of the past, however, doesn't mean that we are to have no recall of the past and the weaknesses that caused our system to develop. To live a healthy life, we actually need to embrace our weaknesses, not ignore or deny them.

When I say we need to embrace our weaknesses, I am not referring to our sins or weakness of character. I am referring to weaknesses of need—those unmet emotional needs caused by neglect and abandonment. And we can deal with these weaknesses in two ways: we can deny them or we can embrace them.

❖ If we choose to deny our weaknesses—as I did for a long time—we will develop a private self which is very different from our public self. Our public self is that part of us that performs, is successful, and wants people to perceive us as strong and without any particular needs. Our private self, however, is that part of us that feels weak, knows our vulnerability, and fears that this vulnerability will be discovered. Our secret self overemphasizes our strengths and covers our weaknesses by exaggeration, boasting, and lies.

Whatever form our weaknesses, we are not to deny them. Such denial is an abandonment of that God-given part of us which needs embracing. And such denial leads to addictive behavior (which can help us feel alive, creative, and powerful—temporarily) and to further shame.

❖ When we embrace our weaknesses—that hidden part of ourselves—we begin to feel whole. Remember, I am not talking about embracing our sin. We are to confess and repent of our sins, but we are to embrace our humanness and our neediness, the part of us that feels weak and vulnerable, the part of us that needs comfort or encouragement, the part of us that is fearful and lonely. These weaknesses can result in emotional distress, immaturity, or the tendency to try to meet our needs in an unhealthy manner. When we embrace them, though, we can deal with our needs in a healthier manner.

## "My Grace Is Sufficient"

The apostle Paul embraced his weakness, that "thorn in the flesh" he refers to in 2 Corinthians 12:7. Paul doesn't explain what the thorn was, but he offers valuable insight as to its possible purpose when he describes it as "a messenger of Satan to buffet me—to keep me from exalting myself!" (12:7).

Three times, Paul prays to God to remove this thorn, but God's response is "My grace is sufficient for you, for power is perfected in weakness" (12:9). Paul concludes that he should glory in his weakness so that the power of Christ might dwell in him. What a tremendous perspective on weaknesses!

Unlike Paul, though, many of us have been ashamed of our weaknesses. But whatever those weaknesses, we are to embrace them just as Paul embraced his. Paul even honored his weakness because he realized that Christ was present in it and that His grace was sufficient.

How can we, like Paul, embrace our weaknesses?

### *Acknowledge Our Weaknesses*

The first step to embracing our weaknesses is to acknowledge them. God gives grace to the humble (James 4:6), and we humble ourselves by admitting that we have needs. These needs may be scars from our childhood, areas where we need to mature, a lack of skills, or a hunger for belonging, purpose, and significance. Whatever our weaknesses, we need to acknowledge them. Also, Scripture instructs us to confess our sins one to another and to pray for one another so that we may be healed (James 5:16). We find strength and freedom in admitting our needs (as well as our sins) to the right person, to someone who will help us and receive us so that we can grow into maturity.

Admitting my needs was difficult for me. Having sexualized my need for physical closeness, I associated that need with my acting out, so needing physical closeness made me feel ashamed and inferior. When I finally admitted my need for physical closeness, I realized that the need itself was not wrong and that I could bring it to my loving heavenly Father. But how embarrassing and awkward it was for me to admit even to Him that I had a need for physical closeness. I needed to touch and to be touched, and I told that to God. The more I acknowledged my needs to God, to other people, and even to myself, the more easily I could embrace that need which had, for so long, felt like a flaw. God's grace was there in my weakness, and His grace was more than sufficient.

### *Accept Our Weaknesses*

Once we acknowledge our weaknesses, we need to accept them; we need to own them. I, for instance, had to accept the emotions of a young boy and a teenager. Part of me had been stuck emotionally at five years old when my drunken father had called me a bastard. As the brunt of his occasional insensitive and untrue jokes about raising another man's child, I was left with a great need to be accepted and loved. I wanted someone to take care of me and to affirm me. As I grew up, I longed to be one of the guys and one of the group. Other emotions were stuck at age five when I was molested by a farmhand. Some emotions were stuck at age twelve when I became a Christian and felt increased rejection from my father. And still other emotions were from my seventeenth year when I felt an ambiguity toward men and a fear of authority because of the awful secret of my molestation.

So during my recovery, I had to embrace the needs of a five-year-old, a twelve-year-old, and a seventeen-year-old. And that meant replaying the nightmarish words of my father who had, in a drunken rage, ordered me to leave home. I had to hear again his curses and his criticisms, his statements that I was not much of a man. Although I could not go back and fix those years, I had to embrace those times of my life and the unmet needs. Only then could I stop responding to those hurts through my secret world of sexual perversion.

But that process of taking ownership of my history was difficult. After grieving my loss, I had vivid pictures of unhappy times throughout my childhood. In one scene, I was standing on the front porch of the house we lived in. I could almost reach out and touch that little boy, his image was so clear to me. With tears, I asked the little boy if he would forgive me for abandoning him and being ashamed of him. I also told him that, with God's help, I would take care of him and that, for the rest of my life, I would be there for him. I wanted the little boy to know that he never again had to be ashamed of his fears and his needs because, by the grace of God, he could be re-parented.

### *Share in the Life of Christ*

Having acknowledged our weaknesses and owned them, we further embrace them by sharing in the life of Jesus Christ and God's grace. I had admitted my needs and I had embraced the very needy little boy inside, but now it was important that I begin to experience the reality of Jesus Christ. My healthy future was not dependent on merely healing the little boy. For my restoration, I needed the life of Jesus Christ within me. I needed to live in the reality of my changed life in Jesus Christ. Not only was I in Jesus Christ, but Jesus Christ was in me (Gal. 2:19-20). With that kind of relationship and faith in the Son of God, I could live a victorious life. I could know that all things work together for the good of them who love Him and for the good of those called according to His purpose (Rom. 8:28). At this point of my restoration, I looked beyond the little boy in me to Jesus Christ in me.

### *Glory in Weakness*

Again, we look to the apostle Paul for an example of this fourth step of embracing our weakness. Like Paul, we are to glory in our weakness because it is an opportunity for God's strength to be made manifest in us. We give honor to the thing about us which was weak and which we despised when we surrender it to God.

I was invited to speak to a group of 200 men, and I was afraid. What if these men didn't think I was masculine enough? Or, worse, what if they knew what a failure I was? I was sure that if I shared out of my weakness, most of the men would get up and walk out. But, to my complete amazement, that didn't happen. Let me share what did happen.

I must confess that, at first, pride entered in, and I told them about some of my past accomplishments like the successful church I had ministered in, the friends I have who played professional football, and the fact that I had attended a junior college on a basketball scholarship (I didn't mention that we didn't win any games that year). I supposed that my audience would identify with me and think of me as one of the guys, but there wasn't any truth in this approach.

As I stood before the men, it seemed as if the Lord was telling me to humble myself and to reveal my weaknesses. God wasn't telling me to be foolish and to share all that was in my heart, but He was telling me to be more open and honest. As I listened to the Holy Spirit, I began to share with the men some of the hurts and fears that I had. I told them about some of the unmet needs I had tried to fulfill through sexual and emotional addiction. I had no idea how they would respond to this, but when my talk ended, the men came forward until there wasn't enough time to minister to everyone. That day I learned that my strength in life and in ministry was to be the strength of Christ perfected in my weakness.

Interestingly, despite all my years of leading a successful church ministry, I have never been asked to speak on church growth. What God has used most in my life is not what I would have considered my strengths or successes. Instead, it has been out of my failures that the love and power of Jesus Christ have been revealed. When people look at me, they do not glory in my strength, but they glory in the power and majesty of God's grace in my life.

### *Glory in the Cross of Christ*

Paul, the man with the thorn in his flesh, writes to the churches of Galatia, "May it never be that I should boast, except in the cross of our Lord Jesus Christ, through which the world has been crucified to me, and I to the world" (6:14). And may that be my vow too!

Even as Christ began to restore me and I began to experience many blessings—including a new ministry beyond anything I could ever imagine—the Holy Spirit reminded me that I was to glory in my weakness. I was never to boast of anything but the Cross. I was not even to boast about my restoration, my recovery, or my healing. I was only to boast about the Cross, for it was the Cross that crucified me to the world and enabled me to love Christ instead. It was Christ's redeeming embrace of mercy that pulled me out of the fire of addiction.

I thought again of Paul. It was Paul who murdered Christians and sought to destroy the church. Yet his zealousness to destroy the church became a zealousness for the Lord of the church and a desire to share the gospel throughout the known world.

Then there was Peter whose mouth was always getting him into trouble. After claiming that he'd follow Christ to prison and even to death, he denied to a servant girl even knowing the Master. Yet out of that same mouth came the sermon on Pentecost that led thousands of souls to Christ.

And John, the Son of Thunder, had cried out for fire from heaven to destroy those who do not receive Christ (Luke 9:54). Yet John became the apostle of love and the one to whom Christ committed His mother. And it was John who saw the revelation of Jesus in all of His glory, a revelation of the incredible love that the Father and the Son share.

God does indeed bring glory to Himself through the weaknesses of His people, and I thank Him that I have tasted that myself.

## Amazing Grace

To accept our weaknesses is to accept our limitations not as permanent but, with the touch of God's grace, changeable. If a limitation happens to be unchangeable as Paul's was, then we can accept God's promise that He will bring meaning and purpose to whatever effects it may have on our life.

I remember deciding that I would never again be ashamed of the little boy who had been so lonely, so hungry for acceptance and human touch. As I looked at several photographs of me as a child, I recognized the potential of that little boy. This realization also helped me let go of the shame I had carried for so long. Then, as I've shared, by the grace of God, I released my natural father and forgave him. I could now trust God my Father to minister to me and even through me.

As we embrace our unmet needs and our human limitations, Christ's strength is made perfect. The grace of God is always sufficient. His grace will supply us, complete us, and transform our very weaknesses into ministry, purpose, and glory for His name.

### *Your Own Story*

- *I use the word* weakness *to refer to our unmet emotional needs. With that definition in mind, list the weaknesses you have a hard time acknowledging and accepting. You don't have to show your list to anyone, but I would encourage you to share the items with your heavenly Father. He alone is able to meet those needs.*
- *Review the section "Glory in Weakness." When have your sins, your failures, or your unmet needs been a chance for the love and power of Jesus Christ to be revealed? Be as specific as you can, and then spend a few minutes thanking God for making His presence so real in your life.*
- *How might your weaknesses (your unmet needs) or your past failures be opportunities for ministry? Ask the Lord to show you, talk to people who know you and your spiritual gifts, and know that God never fails to respond to a sincere, "Here I am, Lord."*

CHAPTER ❦ TEN

# Releasing Unhealthy Shame

*During elementary school, I lived to walk forward and receive my perfect attendance award each June. I realized years later that that piece of paper covered, at least for a moment, the deep-seated shame that I felt inside. It wasn't that I had made mistakes and was embarrassed about them. That would have been a healthy shame. Instead, the shame I felt was the belief that I was a mistake. That unhealthy shame inside me made me strive for acceptance. Even as a child, I was performance-oriented; I looked for things I could do to win acceptance. My goal of perfect attendance—which I reached for seven years—was just one of many ways throughout my life that I tried to avoid the exposure of failure. What if people realized what I already knew—that I was a mistake? I couldn't risk further rejection and abandonment.*

Since the very beginning of my restoration, I have experienced a deep sense of God's grace and love. During the process of repentance, the healthy shame and guilt I felt as I confessed my sin began to lift from my heart. God's forgiveness served as a bridge that ended the isolation from Him and others I had long felt. God stood at my side as I grieved my losses, and He enabled me to embrace my weaknesses. Despite these freeing touches of grace, another type of shame—a shame lodged deep within me—remained.

During the past several years, I have come to understand this shame that bound me and how to become released from it. I began to understand more clearly the words of the apostle Paul in 2 Corinthians—"we have renounced the things hidden because of shame" (4:2). That phrase gripped my heart. I had created a whole hidden world because of the shame that grew out of my childhood fear of being rejected, of being exposed and abandoned. And this kind of unhealthy shame—the most devastating emotion I know—has ensnared and crippled multitudes.

## What Is Shame?

Webster's defines *shame* as "a painful emotion caused by consciousness of guilt, shortcoming, or impropriety." Key to understanding shame, though, is recognizing that there are two types.

❖ Healthy Shame—This type of shame enables us to say, "I made a mistake," "I sinned," and "I am responsible for my actions." We experience a healthy sense of shame when we have done something wrong. We acknowledge our error or our sin, and we learn from our mistake.

Sometimes when we're experiencing healthy shame, we feel shy or embarrassed, and we may even blush. The experience that brings on these reactions reminds us of our limitations and helps us remember that we are not God. Unlike Him, we make mistakes.

And we often need other people or the revelation of the Holy Spirit to help us learn from our failures and mistakes. Failure to learn from our mistakes can lead to callousness, a desensitized conscience, and ultimately shamelessness.

❖ Unhealthy Shame—If we are feeling an unhealthy sense of shame, we have thoughts like, "I'm a mistake" and "I'm flawed and unworthy." Healthy shame comes because of something we have done, but unhealthy shame comes because of something done to us.

Unhealthy shame can manifest itself in two ways. It can make us feel either less than human or more than human. The less-than-human response says, "If I'm a mistake, I can't correct it," and the result is hopelessness. The more-than-human reaction leads to the belief that "I can't afford to make a mistake; I have to be perfect or I'll be rejected." This kind of unhealthy shame leads people to become performance-oriented and, often, to deny their own mistakes and shortcomings. And it is unhealthy shame which I am referring to throughout this chapter.

## Guilt and Shame

One time after I talked about unhealthy shame, someone asked me if we should ever feel legitimate shame or guilt. The answer is yes. We aren't responsible for the unhealthy shame we feel, but we are responsible for how we choose to deal with our unhealthy shame. As believers, we can claim adoption by our heavenly Father, made available to us through Jesus Christ (Gal. 4:5-6; Eph. 1:4-5). Receiving God as "Abba, Father" will open us up to His healing and restoring presence in our lives.

If we do not turn to our heavenly Father to meet our unmet needs, we will then experience legitimate guilt for that wrong decision and the consequences of choosing unhealthy ways to try to meet our needs. This guilt is also partly the result of our bitterness about what caused our unhealthy shame and our unforgiveness of those involved—and that unforgiveness is based in our unbelief that God can use even those events which shamed us to bring glory to Him and benefits to us.

We need to understand the difference between shame and guilt, especially between unhealthy shame and a healthy sense of guilt. The source of guilt is our conscience. Guilt results when, through our words, thoughts, and actions, we violate our values and beliefs. People feeling guilt regret their action, correct their mistake, and learn from it. People feeling unhealthy shame, however, regret who they are; they regret their being rather than their behavior. Furthermore, people who feel unhealthy shame don't see the possibility of correcting the circumstances or especially themselves and thus feel hopeless.

One day our son, Rod, came home from first grade sobbing. When we asked why he was crying, he said that the teacher had called him "a bad apple." Upon further investigation, we learned that the teacher had made a cardboard apple tree for the bulletin board in the front of the classroom. On the tree were thirty paper apples, each one representing a child in the class. When a student received a certain number of marks for talking without permission, his or her apple was removed from the tree, and that student was called "a bad apple." The students whose apples stayed on the tree—the "good apples"—received candy as a prize. Rod, however, had not made the distinction between his behavior and his character. We carefully explained that he was called a bad apple not because of who he was, but because of his wrong actions. With this new insight about his value as a person, Rod, who had been placed at a lower reading level, went to the top of the class within a few weeks and later into a gifted program. He had been freed from shame and freed to excel.

Like Rod, we need to understand the difference between guilt and shame. We also need to understand the difference between guilt and blame. Blame is putting the responsibility for our mistakes on someone else. We blame ourselves when we assume responsibility for someone else's mistakes. This is especially true of young children who have been sexually molested and have carried the guilt of someone else's immorality. These innocent victims carry the shame as well as the blame.

## The Causes of Unhealthy Shame

The causes of unhealthy shame are many and varied. Sadly, a child can be shamed even in the womb. Experts tell us that a child who is not wanted can experience shame even before birth. Shame can also arise from hurtful and traumatic childhood experiences. The disillusionment and hurts of the teenage years can result in shame. Unhealthy shame can result at any point in life when we receive as truth a lie about ourselves and our worth. Shame can come in the daily events of life; it does not always have its seeds in the distant past.

❖ Among the most common causes of unhealthy shame are powerful and hurtful ***words***, phrases, put-downs, nicknames, and name-calling. "You're not worth anything," "You'll be the one in our family to cause the most trouble," "lazybones," "slut"—these few examples suggest the power words can have over us and how they can influence our self-image.

James describes that power by comparing the tongue to fire: "Behold, how great a forest is set aflame by such a small fire!" (3:5). I experienced that power in my own life. As I've shared, when my father was drunk, he would say that I didn't belong to him and call me a bastard. Those words gave me a deep sense of shame.

Even words said in jest can be hurtful (Prov. 26:18-19). I still remember the young couple who attended a social function together not long after being married. The husband made a joke about the size of his wife's nose. Although he didn't mean to hurt her and she laughed at the time, she was deeply wounded and went into a low-grade depression. Her husband's comment had echoed and reinforced comments her family had made while she was growing up. Jokes about appearance, status in life, physical features, nationality, and race can cause shame that lasts a lifetime.

❖ Another cause of shame is ***abuse***, emotional, physical, or sexual. A middle-aged woman who came to see me was overwhelmed by fear, shame, and depression. When she was thirteen years old, an uncle began to molest her—and she had never told anyone. Instead, she had kept her secret and lived out the shame of it in many different ways. Now she was devastated by the consequences.

As we talked, Sandra said that she had always been afraid to tell anyone what had happened to her. When she listened to a teaching on abuse, she realized that she felt shame and guilt because she'd assumed responsibility for what had happened to her. During our conversation, Sandra also acknowledged that she had a real need for affection. She had been raised in an alcoholic home where she never received attention. Through the gifts he bought her and the time he spent with her, this uncle gave her the attention she craved.

I listened to what she said, and then I explained to her that she was only a thirteen-year-old *child* when the abuse took place. Her uncle, in his late twenties, was an authority figure and in a position to protect her. Instead, he had violated her boundaries and victimized her. She had unnecessarily and unhealthily assumed responsibility for his actions; she had felt guilt that wasn't hers. Having blamed herself for an action that was her uncle's fault, she had lived in despair for many years even though she had asked God's forgiveness many times.

With the help of this perspective, Sandra came to accept the fact that she wasn't responsible for the abuse that had happened. She also realized that she was responsible for whether or not she would grieve her loss, forgive her uncle, and release her shame. Her very countenance changed as we spoke. I sensed a marked difference in her as the peace of God descended on her, and she began her journey of restoration.

❖ Shame also arises from ***unmet needs***. According to God's design, each of us has basic human needs (we need closeness, significance, a sense of identity, etc.). When these needs are not met, we often become ashamed of them, and we'll hide them from other people. We may seek to meet our needs through a world of fantasy in which we imagine having our needs met, perhaps based on situations we've observed or experienced in the past. Eventually, we will live out these fantasies and so live out our unmet needs in a secret world which leads to more shame.

❖ ***Mistakes*** and ***failures***—our own, those of people responsible for us, and, as the following story illustrates, those of people we're responsible for—also cause unhealthy shame. If we don't receive God's forgiveness for our actions or if we don't forgive those who have hurt us, we will continue to live in our shame and be bound by it.

Recently, a woman came to talk with me about her son. For years, she had lived with the shame of his lifestyle. Did she remember saying or doing anything that made her feel guilty? Yes, she did. She had been an overprotective mother in a home dominated by an abusive and alcoholic father. She had inappropriately leaned on her son for emotional support, a mistake which she felt forced him into his lifestyle. I listened to her talk, and then I asked her a second question.

Had she asked her son to forgive her for that and for anything she may have done to shame him? Yes, she had done so. In that case, I told her, she was no longer responsible for his shame. I explained that we are responsible for releasing the shame that we put on others, and we do this by asking their forgiveness and God's forgiveness. But we don't need to carry the shame of those who will not be responsible for their own shameful actions. Specifically, this woman needed to assume responsibility for her mistakes and for rebuilding an appropriate relationship with her son, but she was not responsible for her son's choices.

I also told this woman that one of the tactics of the Enemy is to bind us with shame so that we are not free to minister to others. If we are carrying the shame of others, we will not be able to pray or intercede for them. Shame causes us to focus on ourselves in self-pity. Helped by these new insights, this mother began to release her shame and realize that she could love her son and pray for him.

❖ Shame can result when we ***compare ourselves*** to society's standards for such things as physical appearance, social and financial standing, career path, and ethnic background and then decide that we don't measure up. If we look to other people rather than to God's design for us, we can develop an unhealthy shame. Comparisons with other people are based on standards that are meaningless from God's loving and eternal perspective, but not measuring up to those false standards can have a very powerful shaming effect on us.

❖ Other people's ***unrealistic expectations*** for us can also cause shame. While one woman I know was growing up, her mother never allowed her to complete a task. Instead, the young girl was always interrupted by, "Here. Let me do it. You're too slow." When we are given a job beyond our abilities or are made to feel that we're too slow in accomplishing a task, we are victims of unrealistic expectations that cause shame. Also, when we are never affirmed, we sense that we are not quite good enough, and another seed for shame is planted.

❖ ***Embarrassing circumstances*** can cause shame, and the number of possibilities here is enormous. Reading disorders, being corrected in front of others, secrets that were not kept secret, ridicule for our appearance, handicaps or sickness that cause limitations—circumstances and situations like these can cause us great shame.

❖ Finally, ***rejection*** and ***abandonment*** can cause unhealthy shame. This painful rejection can come from parents, siblings, friends, a pastor, or church members. An unwanted pregnancy and unfulfilled promises can also make us feel rejected. We can also learn shame from our parents' use of "the silent treatment" as a part of discipline. Their silence leaves us wondering about ourselves and what we did; their failure to explain what was wrong leaves us feeling flawed.

## The Effects of Shame

Proverbs 16:25 states, "There is a way which seems right to a man, but its end is the way of death." When we have been shamed, however, our perception of the right way to respond to a given situation will be skewed. Shame about who we are can lead to various systems of wrong behavior that result in isolation and loneliness.

❖ One of the most unhealthy effects of shame is the ***false identity*** it can produce in us. We, like Adam and Eve in the Garden (Gen. 3:9-10), will hide ourselves from God and from other people by covering ourselves with false identities. This false identity offers us a false sense of security, a false sense that we're okay.

While I was growing up, I studied hard to make good grades, I struggled to achieve the top score on any project I did, and I went seven years without missing a day of school in order to receive a perfect attendance certificate. I played basketball in high school and then attended a small junior college on a basketball scholarship. At every game, I scanned the crowds looking for my dad's face in hopes of getting his approval—and I never saw him.

My need for acceptance led me to develop a success-oriented system which was later part of my motivation in ministry. Part of me wanted God's best, but another part of me was driven to ***perform for acceptance***. People were drawn to me because of my ministry, but I avoided getting to know them personally. I was convinced that if they really knew me, they couldn't possibly like me.

Our unmet needs may also lead to a system where we appear ***superhuman***. Not wanting to be hurt again or wanting to avoid confrontation with people, we appear more than human. We live apart as one who can never be bothered or angry. My system—my role as a religious leader—enabled me to appear to be a person without needs, a person who has all the answers, a person everyone comes to for solutions to life's problems. Our superhuman system may cast us in the role of family caretaker: we take care of everyone else and neglect ourselves.

In contrast, seeds of shame can also lead to a system where we are the ***scapegoat,*** the person who receives blame for all the problems, the ***victim,*** or the ***self-destructive*** personality. These people sabotage the good things that come into their life and so live out being the loser.

❖ Shame makes us ***unable to accept the blessings God gives***. Recently, for instance, a successful Christian leader called me and said that he was plagued by temptations to which he often succumbed. As

I asked him some questions, we soon discovered a deep shaming experience earlier in his life. Now, even though he was successful, he was living out that shame. Why? He didn't believe that he deserved these blessings; he couldn't believe he deserved this success.

Shame is like a thermostat. Whenever we experience success or blessings, the thermostat of shame will draw us back to shame. Even though shame causes us pain, that pain is familiar and therefore comfortable. That is one reason why someone abused as a child often becomes an abuser or a person raised by an alcoholic often marries an alcoholic. We keep living out our shame; we keep living in our paradoxically painful comfort zone.

❖ Unhealthy shame causes us to ***shame others***. An example from my own life clarifies what I mean. . . . When my children entered junior high, I warned them that if they ever participated in any questionable activity that would embarrass our church fellowship, our family, or the cause of Christ, I would resign the pastorate and take a second job, even if it meant moving to another state. My warning came from my own shame about my secret sin. By issuing that warning, I put my guilt and shame off on my own children instead of dealing with it myself.

Alcoholics do the same thing when they try to make their spouse believe that they are the problem, and they do this when they create a situation to justify their behavior. An angry spouse, for instance, needs a reason to leave the house and/or open the bottle of liquor. The person having an extramarital affair may attempt to make his or her spouse feel unattractive. The person stealing from the company may scrutinize the expense sheets of fellow employees. The minister who rages against the sins of others may actually be covering his own sins. When we do things like this, we are shaming others, and we are responsible for releasing them from the shame we've put on them by asking their forgiveness and by asking God's forgiveness.

❖ Shame *accumulates* as we experience one shameful event after another. An assistant pastor, for instance, told me about making a mistake during an announcement. He laughed because the slip was interesting and funny. Afterwards, however, he went into a depression that seemed out of proportion to his mistake. At this point, though, he remembered times in the past when he had made embarrassing mistakes. When he added his recent mistake to the list of his past mistakes, he experienced the cumulative effects of the mistakes which had caused him shame through the years. Just as unhealthy shame spiraled in his life, it can spiral in ours.

❖ Unhealthy shame *lacks the ability to accept compliments*. "You look nice today!" will be received with, "Oh, my hair looks awful." People who have unhealthy shame simply don't believe that they deserve to be complimented.

❖ Unhealthy shame *seeks death*, both literal and metaphorical. I saw this aspect of shame in my own life when, with the help of a counselor, I realized how I worked to sabotage my ministry. The greater the blessings on my life, the greater my effort to sabotage it, and that effort meant taking greater risks as I satisfied my addiction. This was a form of death that had roots in my belief that I didn't deserve to be blessed or even to live. Ultimately, unhealthy shame leads to suicide—spiritual, moral, or physical.

❖ People carrying the burden of unhealthy shame *lack boundaries*. We who are shamed don't realize that we have dominion in our own lives. We lack the ability to say no. This is especially true of people who have been molested, people whose physical boundaries were violated.

❖ Unhealthy shame results in a *dependence* on other people's opinions, a *fear of being wrong*, a *fear of failure*, and a *fear of confrontation*. Children who are not allowed to have opinions feel shame, and as adults they find it difficult to be confrontive.

❖ Unhealthy shame often leads to a *distrust of authority*, especially spiritual authority. We believe that God can't or won't meet our needs, or we conclude that God doesn't exist and for that reason can't meet our needs. Our fear of being hurt again can lead us to deny spiritual authority. As a result we may become independent, not accountable to anyone, or we may become manipulative of people and circumstances so we won't be hurt.

❖ Unhealthy shame can result in a *fear of intimacy* and an avoidance of relationships. We sabotage friendships and reject people before they can reject us. We operate under the premise that, "If they really knew me, they couldn't possibly love me."

❖ Shame is addictive. As shame keeps acting itself out, those behaviors can develop into *addictions*. Our shame results in certain systems for approaching life, and those systems become our reason for living. Those systems become addictions (see Chapter Six).

Unhealthy shame is at the base of many addictions. The addictive experience grows out of whatever we choose to alter our feelings of shame; the addiction becomes the medication we use so that we don't feel our shame. Our addiction, however, leads us to feel more shame, and we find ourselves trapped in a vicious cycle. This cycle makes us feel even more unworthy, and we turn to our addiction to avoid these feelings.

❖ Shame can lead us to develop ***addictive relationships***. Ashamed of our own being, we look to someone else to become our identity. In an addictive relationship, we . . .

1. Look to someone else for emotional existence. We feel that we can't live without that person.
2. Drop other relationships in order to spend time in the addictive relationship.
3. Become more concerned with that relationship than our relationships with our immediate family members.
4. Focus on sensuality in the relationship.
5. Feel energized when we find others who have a similar bondage.
6. Become exclusive rather than inclusive in the relationship. (In contrast, a healthy relationship has a desire to include others. It wants others to reciprocate in the goodness and the grace of God.)
7. Constantly think about the other person.

A young woman attempted suicide when she discovered that her husband was involved in an affair. Wanda simply felt that she had no reason to live, and her background showed me why. One of several children, she was raised by an alcoholic father and a mother who worked outside the home. Wanda, who lived in constant fear of being alone with her father, was molested by a neighbor when she was a small child. When she told her parents, they scolded her. This incident taught Wanda that no one would take care of her. As an adult, she married a man she believed would take care of her. She thought that he would meet her unmet needs, and so he became her life source. When she found out about his affair, she felt that her life was over. Her reason for being alive was no longer there, so Wanda had wanted to die.

After working with a Christian psychiatrist, Wanda was able to acknowledge her unmet needs and understand how she had staked her identity on her husband. She saw the system of lies she had believed about her value as a person and how she had been living as if those lies were true. As she receives help, Wanda is changing her way of thinking and her actions. She is experiencing restoration.

❖ Similar to the addictive relationship is the ***enmeshing relationship***. Here, two lives become so intertwined that being apart makes the individuals feel disloyal. This relationship is shaming because it keeps us from becoming the unique and separate person what God wants us to become. We can't fulfill His purpose for our life.

A controlling parent can contribute to an enmeshing relationship. We see this when a child becomes an extension of the mother or the father—when the athlete fulfills his father's dream; when the mother lives out her life through her daughter; and when parents push their child into medicine, law, or some other prestigious occupation to fulfill their own unfulfilled fantasies.

Enmeshment also occurs when a sibling substitutes as the mother or father. Consider the older brother or sister who helps take care of the family. This role becomes the basis of their being accepted in the family, but it doesn't allow them the freedom to become what God intends them to be. Today, that older sibling may be a mother or father to a spouse or to other people around them.

❖ Unhealthy shame causes us to ***suppress our feelings***. Tragically, these suppressed feelings will be lived out in further shame. I know from an experience involving my father. The day before his open-heart surgery, I went to see him, and I shared my concern for his soul. Through the years, my dad had claimed to be an unbeliever, and at times he openly expressed hostility toward Christianity. This time, however, he stated that he believed that Jesus was the Son of God, and he acknowledged Jesus Christ as his Lord and Savior. When we prayed, he asked to be forgiven for his sins. I was so overjoyed I could hardly speak. I pictured us traveling and ministering together, the relationship of the past completely healed.

The next day's surgery, however, prompted a stroke, and my father died a year later. As I've said, the emotional and sexual addictions in my life intensified. I had fantasized about sharing a complete relationship with my father, but that fantasy would now never be a reality. In my addiction, I searched for that father-son relationship which was never made complete, and I lived out the shame that was rooted in never having received my father's love. For seven years, I didn't visit my dad's grave. Only when I could finally say good-bye to my dad did I get on with my life.

Recently a woman from the northeastern United States came to me with her unresolved grief. Joan's husband had committed suicide while she was hospitalized, and she hadn't taken part in the funeral service or the burial. Her doctor hadn't allowed it. After two years, Joan was still dealing with depression. Having been raised in a family that didn't express feelings, Joan had learned long ago to hide her feelings. She had repressed the pain and sorrow she had felt at her husband's death, and she was ashamed of her feelings. People were telling her that she was an example of God's strength, but Joan wanted to burst out crying.

As I talked with Joan, she came to understand that we don't have to be ashamed of our pain and sorrow, that these feelings don't have to be suppressed, that they are a part of grief, and that these emotions help us heal. Later, Joan and I met with her pastor, and we had a funeral service for her husband in the pastor's study. The pastor and I then encouraged Joan to visit her husband's grave with a friend and say good-bye to him. When she was able to do that two weeks later, her depression lifted. Joan experienced some closure at the funeral service, she felt her sorrow, and then she released it. She still feels some sadness, but she is able to face the future with new energy and hope.

## Releasing Shame

As long as we believe the lies Satan has perpetrated about God and about us, we will continue to live in our unhealthy shame. We must exchange these lies for the truth as a part of our healing process (see Chapter Five). We need to act on our belief that God created us in His image, in His likeness, and to share in His dominion (Gen. 1:26) and claim the promise that God will supply all our needs (Phil. 4:19). We must also make a conscious effort to release our shame.

1. First, we need to ***ask God to forgive us*** for the shame that we are responsible for (our healthy shame for our mistakes and sins) and for the shame that we have put on others through our cruel words and thoughtless actions. We also need to ask those people whom we have shamed to forgive us.

It is also important that we ask God's forgiveness for our unbelief. Let me explain. If we continue to carry shame about who we are, we are still believing lies about ourselves. We are, for instance, believing other people's statements about us rather than what God has said about His love for us and our value to Him. We must repent of believing those lies which come from Satan; we must choose to believe in the reality of God's unconditional and unlimited love for us.

2. We then need to ***give our shame back to Satan***, the originator of shame, because if we don't give it back, we will give it forward. In other words, we will carry it with us into the future and, consciously or subconsciously, act out that shame in various unhealthy ways.

How do we give back that shame? The world would say through revenge on the person or persons who shamed us, but that is not the way of the believer. Paul tells us in Romans, "Never take your own revenge, beloved, but leave room for the wrath of God, for it is written 'Vengeance is Mine, I will repay,' says the Lord" (12:19).

We who are believers release our shame when we, in the spirit of Christ, forgive those who shamed us. In the presence of a qualified counselor, we can deal with our shame and eventually say, "I give my unhealthy shame to Satan," and we can find freedom through this act of verbalization.

We can also give back our shame through prayer: "Heavenly Father, in the name of Jesus Christ and by the power of His Holy Spirit, I give the unhealthy shame I feel but that is not mine to carry back to Satan. By the authority of Your Name, I receive Your promised destruction of Satan's works. I ask and pray in the name of our Lord Jesus Christ. Amen."

3. We will continue to bear shame that isn't ours until we ***grieve the loss*** we experienced because of sins against us. If some of our losses are due to our parents' actions (this can include abandonment, rejection, physical abuse, and sexual molestation), we need to recognize the sabotage that Satan has worked through families and generations. We do not seek to blame our parents; we seek only the opportunity to release the past and to assume responsibility for God's glory and power in our lives.

And this opportunity comes when we ***forgive*** the person from whom our shame came and so release them from our bitter judgment. We forgive a person from our heart when we no longer hold their offenses against them and no longer desire for them to suffer the consequences of those offenses. We release people from our bitter judgments when we no longer hold them in emotional prisons, thinking of them only in connection with their failure and hurtful actions. When we choose instead to see those who hurt us as God sees them—as fallible human beings who themselves have been hurt—we will no longer want to see them hurt; we will no longer want them to pay the price for their actions. And we will have taken another step toward releasing our unhealthy shame.

## A Word of Hope

What is shame? What causes shame? And what are the effects of shame? Together, we've answered these questions. We've also seen how devastating the burden of shame can be and how powerful a force it can be in our lives. Shame can lead to systems of wrong behavior that result in isolation, loneliness, and even greater shame.

When we begin to understand the roots of our shame, feel the pain of those past events, and see the loss we experienced, we will then be able to change our way of functioning in the world. That's when release from unhealthy shame can come. That's when people burdened by the weight of shame can be freed from its power, freed to live a life of wholeness in Christ, a life of transparency, confidence, and love, a life that will glorify God.

### Your Own Story

- *Review "The Causes of Unhealthy Shame." What causes of unhealthy shame have you experienced? Let the Holy Spirit show you where you need to start the process of forgiving those who hurt you and ask Him to enable you to do so.*
- *Look again at "The Effects of Shame." What effects of unhealthy shame do you see in your life? In prayer and/or with the help of a skilled counselor, give back the shame you've carried. This may involve prayer, forgiveness, and the study of God's Word. The Bible teaches that you are of great value to your heavenly Father, and the Holy Spirit can help you believe that fact and act on it. Know, too, that your heavenly Father will bring healing to those areas of hurt—those effects of shame—which you lay before Him.*
- *You may remember words or phrases from your childhood that hurt you and caused you shame. Are you now doing the same to others? Spend a few minutes thinking about the words which you speak, the banter in your family, the nicknames you have for one another, and the patterns of your teasing. Confess where you have been shaming someone. Ask God's forgiveness and that person's forgiveness. Also ask the Holy Spirit to help you control your tongue so that you won't speak thoughtless and hurtful words.*

# CHAPTER ELEVEN

# Renewing the Spirit and Restoring the Soul

*As I was driving home one evening after a very disappointing and disillusioning experience, memories of an old sin pattern from the past began to resurface. I had used that pattern of behavior as a kind of medication for my emotions in times of loneliness, anger, shame, and disappointment. These visual images in my mind were vivid and compelling. Those actions could still provide the comfort they always had, couldn't they? The attraction of my past way of dealing with the pain I was now feeling was overwhelming. I knew those actions would not be healthy or godly, but just knowing didn't seem to be enough to help me fight the power of my addiction.*

nformation alone will not change our life. Revelation in our spirit is what produces change. In fact, that is how a friend of mine differentiates between information and revelation. He says, "When you have revelation in your spirit, there will be immediate change."

I used to think that enough information would change my life. Desperately searching for an answer to my sexual addiction, I read several books a week. (Before we moved, I gave away twenty-one boxes of them!) Books were a painkiller for me when I couldn't deal with the hurt inside. I knew a lot about the problems that I struggled with, but that knowledge alone didn't have the power to change my life. Instead, I felt more guilty because I had all this understanding, but I still hadn't changed.

Then, as I studied Romans, I discovered that the word *renew* in Romans 12:2—"Do not be conformed to this world, but be transformed by the renewing of your mind . . ."—is different from the word *renew* in Ephesians 4:23-24—"Be renewed in the spirit of your mind, and put on the new self . . ." The word *renew* in Romans means "to make new" as in "to make different"; in Ephesians, *renew* means "to make recent." That difference, as subtle as it may seem, is important to the restoration process.

## Spirit and Soul

Scripture makes a distinction between spirit, soul, and body. In 1 Thessalonians 5:23, for instance, Paul writes, "May the God of peace Himself sanctify you entirely; and may your spirit and soul and body be preserved complete, without blame at the coming of our Lord Jesus Christ." And the distinction between spirit and soul is important.

❖ Our spirit is that part of us that is sensitive to and knows God. Our spirit contains our conscience, that part of us by which the Lord searches our inner being. When we become Christians, our spirit is born again. Our spirit becomes the candle of the Lord: in our spirit, the light of God now dwells (Col. 1:27). Having been quickened and joined to the Lord, our spirit does not need to be made different (one meaning of the word *renew*). Instead, "be renewed in the spirit" (Eph. 4:23-24) means to be made aware of what God is saying in the present tense (*renew* meaning to be made recent). When we live in the reality of God's presence—of who He is in us and what He is saying to us in our spirit from minute to minute—we are renewed and strengthened in our inner person.

❖ Our soul includes our mind, will, and emotions. When we become Christians, however, our soul does not become born again. Our mind, will, and emotions are not suddenly created new. Since our soul is not born again when we put our faith in Jesus, we who are believers are charged to not let our soul be conformed to the world, to the evil systems of thought and patterns of life (Rom. 12:2). We are to be "transformed by the renewing of [our] mind" (Rom. 12:2), and "mind," from the Greek word *nous,* refers to our decision-making process and therefore to our lifestyle, actions, and opinions. The Bible teaches us that we are to be renewed in the sense of being made different. We are to be changed to be in conformity to the life of Christ in our spirit. For that to happen, our soul needs to be re-anchored, and that's where our faith comes in. The hope which we now have in Christ can be an anchor for our changeable mind, will, and emotions, an anchor for our changeable soul (Heb. 6:19).

The three stages of marriage illustrate how this anchoring and re-anchoring can affect us. The first stage in marriage is the romance or "wine-and-dine" stage. It is a time of excitement, a time of creating good memories together. Next comes the stage of disillusionment where bad memories seem to outnumber good ones. When the bad starts to outweigh the good, the soul gets anchored in the negative; we get stuck in the bad memories. Helen and I went through this stage after my exposure: I had let her down and hurt her deeply. She was understandably disillusioned about our marriage—but, thankfully, we didn't stay here. The third stage is transformation, and Helen and I experienced this once we were no longer anchored in the bad memories of the disillusionment stage. We found a new house in Florida, and we had a lot of fun together just cleaning house and shopping. Forgiveness in our relationship prevented bitterness from taking root, and our new memories gave us a stronger anchor for our relationship. From that point, whenever I thought about our marriage, I automatically thought about all the good things that were happening.

Re-anchoring our soul—as Helen and I re-anchored our marriage—can be a difficult and lengthy process. I remember Susan, a woman who was terrified of the freeway. When she was a child, she and her family took a trip that was the fulfillment of a long-held dream for them. While they were in the car, Susan and her sister started fighting, and Susan's father turned around and, without warning, hit her. Susan was terrified. She had knots in her stomach for the rest of the trip, and this powerful memory stayed lodged not just in her mind but in her emotions.

Several years later, whenever Susan drove home from college, she took back roads even though it added several hours to the trip. She knew she couldn't go on like this. She wanted to change; she wanted to move on from being anchored in bad memories of freeway driving. So I asked Susan what God's desire for her was. When she said that she could see herself just curling up in the car reading her Bible, I told her that she needed to have a trusted friend be her driver while she rode in the car and read her favorite passage. I wanted her to experience the joy of devotion with Jesus on the freeway. The first time she rode down the freeway, she broke into a sweat, but the second time she got the Word into her and it was a wonderful experience. She repeated this exercise again and again, and by doing so, she began to anchor her soul with good memories.

## Imagination: Bringing Old Memories to Light

In his first epistle, Peter reminds us of our need to control our soul when he writes, "Gird your minds for action, keep sober in spirit, fix your hope completely on the grace to be brought to you at the revelation of Jesus Christ" (1:13) There is a battle for our soul, for our mind, will, and emotions. We need, therefore, to be in control of our passions and our imagination; we need to change our soul so that we can be sensitive and obedient to the leading of the Holy Spirit. We need to gird the loins of our mind with God's truth and His reality.

Changing our soul will also change our actions because, I believe, all actions are birthed in our imagination. (When lust is conceived, for example, it brings forth sin, and sin always brings forth death.) And our imagination is triggered through, among other things, our sight and hearing.

When I was lonely, angry, upset, disappointed, or feeling shame, I medicated my pain with wrong actions that were addictive and that had usually been prompted by a visual temptation of some sort. I remember seeing specific objects and certain images, and I knew these needed to be changed. I knew I needed to gird my mind for action, but I didn't know how to do this. Visual temptation was coming at me from every direction.

One night I ran to Jesus. Fixing my hope completely on His grace, I cried out to Him and shared with Him what was happening to me. When I prayed, "Jesus, I don't know how to deal with this! Show me Your reality!," a powerful thing happened to me. Suddenly, all I could see was a picture of what I had acted out before. I didn't try to hide my sinfulness from Jesus. Instead, I looked at my actions in the light of Jesus, and I realized that it wasn't my new nature in Christ to do what I was doing. Satan would like for us to believe that our memories of our wrong actions reflect who we really are, but I claimed the words of Paul in Romans 7—"I am no longer the one doing it, but sin which dwells in me" (v. 20). I accepted what Paul said as truth: those actions did not reflect who I am in Jesus Christ.

## Being Anchored in the Mind of the Lord

Jesus taught me much about myself when I brought my temptations, my memories, and my imaginings from the past into His light. Rather than denying my struggle, I shared it with my Savior, and He helped me realize that my sinful addiction had been my way of meeting my needs from the past. And the more I dismantled my systems, the more clearly I saw that I had learned those systems from the past with all its unmet needs and hurtful experiences. Each of us brings hurts from the past into our Christian life, but Jesus enables us to replace those lies and counterfeits with the reality of His truth, love, and provision.

When I brought my old memories to light, for instance, the Holy Spirit showed me a needle being pushed into my veins and said that my addiction was a fix that would lead to destruction. With that image, God let me see the reality of what I was dealing with, and then He gave me a vision for my future. I saw myself ministering to a multitude of people, and I realized that my earlier ministry had been an addiction as well. The Holy Spirit also told me that this future ministry was what Satan wanted to steal from me by holding up the temporary medication of my addiction to ensnare me. I laid hold of God's promise and asked Him to help me reorder my soul and strengthen me so that I wouldn't succumb to the temptation of the pleasurable but deadly medication of my addiction. This vision was part of the process of reanchoring my soul.

Wanting to become better anchored in the Word, I spent more time reading the Bible and I even memorized chapters of Scripture. I also read through the books of the prophets, a section of the Bible which I had avoided because of its harsh tone. As God led me through the prophets, however, I began to know better the character and the heart of my heavenly Father. Pages that had long been very uncomfortable reading material now revealed to me God's severe mercy and His heart for restoration. I saw the love of God in a new way: His judgments were a way of protecting us from ourselves. The reanchoring of my soul was happening.

## A Dulled Spirit

As I've said, our spirit is that part of us that is sensitive to and knows God, and our spirit contains our conscience. The Holy Spirit quickens us to be aware of God's presence and His leading, but our spirit can become defiled and our sensitivity to God dulled.

❖ Our spirit can become dulled when, after being hurt, we allow the root of bitterness to spring up.

❖ Our spirit can become dulled when we act according to the whims of the flesh rather than in obedience to God's commands. Such actions start hardening us to the things of God.

❖ Our spirit can also become dulled whenever we start believing a lie about God or ourselves instead of the truth. Behind every sin pattern is a system of lies, and behind every lie there is THE lie that God isn't good and He won't take care of us.

A couple I once talked to, for example, was deeply depressed because of their finances. Convinced that depression comes from believing a lie, I suggested that they had believed the lie that money ultimately gives happiness. They were turning to finances to make them happy instead of to God. Other people believe the lie that God is not big enough to meet their needs, and that kind of lie about God can separate us from our heavenly Father.

I know from experience that lies can separate us from God. I believed my father's lie that I would never amount to anything. Not a Christian, my father would curse anything to do with Jesus. Many times he kept me from church by making me work. One night, he approached me in a drunken rage, cursing about Christ and telling me that in the morning he wanted me to leave the house. Only seventeen years old, I cried and cried, hoping that he would come into my room and tell me that he didn't mean it—but he didn't.

I had just spent my last dollar on a tire for my old car, so I had no money to take with me. As I gathered my clothes, I kept wanting my father to come tell me not to leave. Still he didn't, so I left home. I washed dishes, sacked groceries, and worked for farmers. Even though I received a scholarship to college where I played basketball and met Helen, those were dark days, and in that darkness my father's words echoed through my mind—"You're not much of a man." I played basketball and was president of my class, but I never let anyone get close to me because I believed the lie that I wasn't much of a man. If I let people get close to me, they might find out that I wasn't worth much. My father's lie defiled my spirit and dulled my sensitivity to God.

## Renewing the Spirit: Confession and Repentance

But a defiled spirit can be cleansed; a dulled sensitivity to God can be sharpened. The cleansing comes when we confess our sin to God. We must confess the lies about God we believed and the sinful acts, the mistrust, and the separation from God which those beliefs resulted in. After we ask God to forgive us, we must repent and change our ways.

Changing our ways means re-anchoring our soul. We must replace lies with the truth of God's Word. We must look to God to meet our needs rather than to our familiar and possibly addictive systems. We must be willing to cooperate with God to take these steps of change, but our willpower alone will not enable us to succeed.

Bob came to talk to me about a problem he was having with lust. He lived near a beach, but he felt that he couldn't even walk along the shore because of his problem. Bob needed to re-anchor his soul in fellowship with Jesus, so I suggested that Bob take his Bible to the beach with him and begin to memorize Scripture. As Bob meditated on God's Word, I believed that he would begin to associate his time at the beach with his relationship with God and that he would go to the beach with the intent of sharing the Lord. Also, I encouraged Bob to generalize his feelings instead of sexualizing them: I encouraged him to view a woman as a recipient of God's love rather than an object of lust. Over a period of months, Bob was able to re-anchor his soul in Jesus. He relied on the power of the Spirit to overcome the evil power of lust with good.

## Renewing the Spirit: Revelation

The cleansing of our spirit also comes when we stop living off the fumes of something that happened in the past—six days ago, six months ago, or longer. We need to live in the present. We need to hear what the spirit of God is saying today. Otherwise we are going to be living according to a set of rules based on a lie and leading to death.

And how do we know what God is saying today? By walking in daily fellowship with Christ, developing a consistent prayer life, hiding God's Word in our hearts, being in fellowship with other Christians, and listening for God's revelations to us. And how do we receive revelation? We receive revelation in our spirit when we ask for it. But be warned—these revelations in your spirit will call for changes in your life, just as the Spirit's revelation changed the lives of the disciples.

Consider how the disciples came to Jesus. I don't think they would have given up their livelihood and followed Jesus if they hadn't known that He was the Christ, Son of the living God. When Jesus asked Peter who He was, Peter answered that He was the Christ of the living God (Matt. 16:15-17). Jesus responded by saying that flesh and blood hadn't revealed this to him. Instead, Peter's understanding was based on a revelation from God the Father. And the more revelation that the disciples received about Jesus, the more their lives were changed.

When I started getting revelations, I had to start changing a lot of things in my soul. I had to get new information; I learned more about God and got rid of my distorted ideas. I had to start associating with certain people, and God allowed new friends to come into my life. I had to ask forgiveness for believing a lie and work on re-anchoring my soul in God. All of this has been part of my transformation. When God revealed to me who I really am and who He is in me, transformation started happening fast.

## Receiving God's Revelation

We receive a fresh revelation from God when we ask for it, and that recent revelation of His goodness, His love, and His purpose for us is what changes us.

In Scripture—a blessed revelation of God—we see various expressions of who Jesus is. To those of us with physical needs, Jesus is the Healer. For those with financial needs, Jesus is the One who provides, the One who breaks the loaves and fishes and multiplies them. To some of us, Jesus comes as the God of mercy, the God of all hope. To others, He comes as the God who judges or the Father or the Savior. Jesus reveals Himself through many different expressions of His grace.

And sometimes God reveals Himself by giving us a spirit of wisdom, the ability to sense the loss or gain of God's glory. Once when I was talking to a man who was caught up in sin, I realized that he needed wisdom, but he didn't have any sense of loss. He didn't even think that he'd be caught in his sin, and he rested secure in the lie that there wouldn't be any negative results from his sin if he were never caught. But the truth is that God is aware of our actions and that there are spiritual consequences for our sinful deeds whether we know it or not. This man was deceiving himself with earthly wisdom and a temporal viewpoint. What he needed was divine wisdom that would enable him to see how his actions meant the loss of God's glory in the spiritual realm. After ongoing counseling and help in uncovering his false belief system, this man experienced restoration and is now ministering to people who struggle as he once did.

Like this man I counseled with, each of us needs understanding and wisdom, or life will be confusing. Several years ago, I attended a conference on sexual addiction. One night during the conference, I saw in a dream a man whom I had totally blocked from my mind. This man had molested me when I was growing up, and suddenly I felt the anger, hurt, and rage of that moment. I also saw that those with whom I had been involved in my sexual addiction in some way resembled the man in this dream. It was uncanny; it was diabolical. But God gave me a spirit of understanding—a revelation—so that I could see how the Enemy had been working in my life. This understanding and insight helped me as I continued on my journey of restoration.

## God's Revelation and Our Point of Need

Through the years I've noticed some very important things about what God reveals about Himself:

❖ God's revelations to us will never contradict the character or nature of God.

❖ God's revelations will always harmonize with the teachings of the Bible.

❖ God's revelations will express an aspect of His character that corresponds to our point of need. Consider Jesus' letters to the seven churches in the book of Revelation (1-3). Each letter expresses an aspect of God's character which especially meets the needs of the particular church being addressed. Still today, God will meet us at our point of need when He reveals Himself to us.

❖ Furthermore, God's revelations to us are in accordance with the sevenfold spirit of God revealed in Isaiah 11. There we read a prophecy about Jesus Christ: "The Spirit of the LORD will rest on Him, the spirit of wisdom and understanding, the spirit of counsel and strength, the spirit of knowledge and the fear of the LORD" (v. 2). Note the sevenfold expressions of God's Spirit:

❖ The Spirit of the Lord—Sometimes the mere presence of Jesus will mean bondage broken. Remember the woman who reached out to touch the hem of Jesus' garment? She found freedom from her longtime disease (Matt. 9:20-22). Even for us today, an awareness of the awesome and gracious presence of Jesus lets us know that God is there for us, and often that intimacy gives freedom and healing.

❖ The spirit of wisdom—Wisdom is the discernment of loss and gain for the kingdom of God. With wisdom, we see life—our actions, our decisions, our activities and their consequences—from an eternal perspective. This expression of God's spirit will enable us to make wise choices.

❖ The spirit of understanding—The psalmist confesses being envious of the wicked "until I came into the sanctuary of God; then I perceived their end" (73:17). A revelation in the sanctuary gave the psalmist an understanding of events, and we can receive that same spirit of understanding today. When God reveals Himself, we can gain an understanding of how something happened and why; we can see the cause-and-effect relationship between occurrences; we can be enlightened about what is happening around us.

❖ The spirit of counsel—Often God's revelation will give us a sense of knowing His will for us, His direction, His purpose for our life, and His plans for us. This is the spirit of counsel, and it enables us to continue strong and confident in our walk of faith.

❖ The spirit of might—At times we may need an awareness of God's power and strength. God may meet us at a point of need by showing us His might and enabling us to clearly see His hand in our life. God may reveal Himself through an unusual demonstration of His power in the form of answered prayer.

❖ The spirit of knowledge—Knowing the ways of God—His character, how He moves and works in people's lives and in history—can be a revelation at our point of need. Sometimes the spirit of knowledge will also mean knowing something without having previously learned it. Either way, the insight is evidence of God in our life.

❖ The fear of the Lord—God may reveal to us His authority, His position, and His power. We can only respond in reverent awe and fear. A revelation of God's authority will remind us that He is in control of our life and of the world.

Note that, in his prayer for revelation in Ephesians 1:15-23, Paul also refers to the sevenfold expressions of the Spirit of God (see the chart at the end of this chapter).

God wants to be known by His people, and He can make Himself known through very personal revelations to each one of us. And in those revelations, He graciously and lovingly meets us at a point of need.

## Restoring the Soul

Renewal must take place in our spirit before restoration can take place in our soul. Once we are walking closely with Jesus, He can work in our lives to transform our soul—our mind, will, and emotions—into His image. Several symbols from Scripture reveal what this restoration involves (see the chart at the end of this chapter):

❖ ROOTS
We need to be ***re-rooted*** in God's love if our actions, words, and thoughts are to be salt and light in this world (Eph. 3:17). God's Word and His Spirit will provide the nutrients and life-giving water for our mind, will, and emotions just as the roots of a plant provide it with what it needs to live.

❖ ANCHOR
Just as an anchor gives stability and offers reliable and secure support, the hope of the gospel gives us the anchor we need for the storms of life (Heb. 6:17-20). We need to be ***re-anchored*** from the despair of life without Jesus Christ to the hope He offers—hope which guarantees our safety during the journey of life.

❖ BOND
A bond is that which binds, fastens, and holds. Immoral relationships, dependent emotional relationships, enmeshed family relationships, unresolved grief, blind loyalty to an organization or denomination, unfor-

giveness, idolatry, devotion to Satan—these are inappropriate bonds for our soul. We who are in the process of restoration need to be ***re-bonded*** with God (Rev. 19:5) and with fellow believers (Heb. 10:25).

❖ PARENT

Parents are a child's original caretakers, the ones chosen to bring the child into the world and meet his or her basic emotional, physical, and spiritual needs. Sadly, this relationship is often the source of many of the hurts and abandonment issues that people carry into adulthood. We therefore need to release the past, embrace our hurting inner child, and receive the spirit of adoption from our heavenly Father and the blessing of His church as our extended family. When we cry out to "Abba, Father!," we can be ***re-parented*** by Him (Rom. 8:15).

❖ GIRD

To gird means to encircle or fasten with a belt, a sign of preparing oneself for action. We are to let go of those feelings and thoughts which filled our mind as unbelievers. We are to ***re-gird*** our minds for action for God by focusing on Him (1 Pet. 1:13).

With new sensitivity to God and a new means of knowing His love, we can walk in His light, guided by His revelations to our spirit.

With a new source of life, a new anchor, a new bond, a new Father, and a new focus on God's truth, we are ready to be restored in our soul and bring glory to God through our mind, will, and emotions.

## *Your Own Story*

- *Your Spirit—Your spirit is the part of you that is sensitive to and knows God. What would you like to do to know God better or to become more sensitive to His presence in your life? Set yourself a specific goal and ask a friend to hold you accountable.*
- *God's Revelation—When has God revealed His love for you in a very personal way? When has He made His will for you unmistakably clear? Write down the specifics of one of God's revelations to you. Let it be a touchstone of faith as you now ask Him for another revelation of His love or His will.*
- *Your Soul—Your soul is your mind, will, and emotions. In your opinion, what aspect of your soul needs renewal, needs to be made different and more in conformity with Jesus Christ? Choose one of the five images of restoration and set yourself a specific goal for renewing your soul. Know that God will bless your desire to be more Christlike.*

## The Sevenfold Expressions of the Spirit of God

| Isaiah 11:1-3 | Ephesians 1:15-23 |
|---|---|
| Spirit of the Lord | "Revelation in the knowledge [intimate awareness] of Him" |
| Spirit of wisdom | "Spirit of wisdom" |
| Spirit of understanding | "The eyes of your heart may be enlightened" |
| Spirit of counsel | "The hope of His calling" |
| Spirit of might | "The surpassing greatness of His power" |
| Spirit of knowledge | "Revelation in the knowledge of Him" |
| Fear of the Lord | "All things in subjection under His feet" |

## Restoring the Soul: Biblical Images of Restoration

| *To* | | *From* |
|---|---|---|
| | **Root** | |
| Root of Bitterness<br>Heb. 12:15 | | Rooted and grounded in love<br>Eph. 3:17 |
| Tree of the knowledge of good and evil<br>Gen. 2:17 | | Tree of life<br>Rev. 2:7 |
| | **Anchor** | |
| Despair<br>Psalm 42 | | Hope<br>Heb. 6:17-20 |
| | **Bond** | |
| Inappropriate bonding<br>Col. 2:18-19<br>Isaiah 58:6 | | Appropriate bonding<br>Rev. 19:5 |
| | **Parent** | |
| Abandonment<br>Psalm 27:10 | | Acceptance<br>Romans 8:15 |
| | **Gird** | |
| Error<br>Eph. 4:25 | | Truth<br>1 Peter 1:13 |

CHAPTER ❦ TWELVE

# Restoration: An Issue of the Heart

*"O God, I want to be a man after your own heart." Like King David, this was my heart cry, but I soon learned that I could not become God's person on my own power. I was not able to do the spiritual heart surgery required. After trying but failing to become the person I knew God wanted me to be, I learned that Christ is the Great Physician. He alone is able to cleanse and purify our heart by His indwelling presence and His lordship in our life.*

estoration is an issue of the heart. Our relationship with Jesus—although we may talk about steps and rules and things we ought to do—is also ultimately a relationship of the heart. And in this journey toward healing, restoration, and joy, these two matters of the heart come together: Our restoration depends on our relationship with Jesus.

First of all, what is the heart?

❖ Our heart is our real self, an expression of our spirit and our soul. Our heart is who we really are, and it reflects what we really believe. Our heart is the collection of our values, affections, desires, and dreams. Our heart is the root of our passions and our values.

❖ As keeper of our passions and our values, our heart determines our decisions. (Show me a person's decisions and I will know much about that person's heart.) We are to direct our heart toward God so that our decisions will be in line with His will for us.

❖ The value system of our heart is based on what we believe. If we believe a lie about God, then our value system will not be based on the God of heaven and His standards. If we believe a lie, we will live according to a wrong value system: we will build our life around and give glory to whatever seems to meet our deepest needs. If we believe the truth about God and about ourselves, though, we will have a right value system: we will be living our life for Jesus Christ.

❖ Jesus wisely observed that "where your treasure is, there will your heart be also" (Matt. 6:21). We can't separate our value system from our heart.

❖ Scripture tells us that when we are born-again, not only do we receive a new spirit, but we receive the spirit of Jesus Christ in us. Our spirit is made alive and joined to the Lord. The Lord gives us a new heart, a heart passionate for Him and committed to His purposes. If we are not a new creation, we are not going to have this passion for Jesus.

## A Heart Void of God's Truth

Unbelievers do not have a love of God's truth in their heart (2 Thess. 2:10). As a result, they have erroneous beliefs about God and, because it is based on those beliefs, a wrong value system. Their wrong concept of God results in an idolatrous value system.

❖ Consider people who grew up in poverty and went without many material comforts and even everyday necessities. Some of these people may believe the lie that if they are ever going to be happy, it will be because of more money. More money can be helpful, but money isn't what makes us happy. The world is full of wealthy but miserable people.

The Lord wants His people to prosper, but being prosperous is not the same as being rich (3 John 2). We are rich when we hoard what we have and don't give to others in need. Prosperity, however, is having enough and giving to those in need. Without this understanding, we can easily accept the lie that money will make us happy. We may think that riches will mean an end to our suffering, and we'll never learn that Christ is the only true source of security. Our heart will be set on the acquisition of things rather than on the kingdom of God.

❖ People who were not accepted when they were growing up will often believe the lie that if they were more important, had the right kind of job, or looked a certain way, then they would be accepted and happy. There is nothing wrong with a good job, an acceptable appearance, or even an amount of prestige, but when we believe that these things will make us happy, we are believing a lie. And, instead of seeking the kingdom, we live a form of idolatry in our quest for status and importance.

## A Heart for God

A life lived in God's presence and according to His values is known by the fruit it bears, and Paul writes that "the fruit of the Spirit is love, joy, peace, patience, kindness, goodness, faithfulness, gentleness, self-control" (Gal. 5:22-23), fruit which has eternal significance. We bear such fruit when we seek—as our top priority—Jesus, His kingdom, and His righteousness (Matt. 6:33). We find real happiness when Christ is in us. God is love, and so in Him we find the love we've longed to receive. We also find joy and peace.

But not everyone accepts God's values; not all of us wholeheartedly seek His kingdom. This is because our needs can determine our values. An immature value system will be based upon what brings us pain or pleasure. A mature value system will be based upon what will bring glory to God and increase to His kingdom. Our values will either be based on what begins to meet our needs or on what will bring glory to God. Some of us are in between—and we are in the process of being purified.

## A Heart of Joy

Along with a heart for God, believers will be blessed with the fullness of joy, and our relationship with God is fundamental to that joy.

❖ King David learned that "In Thy presence is fulness of joy" (Psalm 16:11). Have you ever felt a full and unspeakable joy? There have been times in my life when I have felt the presence of the Lord so strongly that I just wanted to bask in it. And such times in His presence lead to a greater intimacy with Jesus and a clearer understanding of who I am but, more importantly, of who Christ is. This knowledge brings a fullness of joy and a freedom from what people think about me. I am free to genuinely love people because my worth comes from being accepted by the Beloved. His presence frees me to love and frees me to be joyful.

❖ We experience fellowship with the Father by having a relationship with Christ (1 John 1:3-4), and that fellowship will result in joy. When we have a right relationship with the Father, our whole value system begins to change, and we are able to see other people as having great value.

❖ In the Psalms, David also writes, "Delight yourself in the LORD; and He will give you the desires of your heart" (37:4). David is not saying that we will get anything and everything we want. He is saying that, as we enter into a relationship with the Lord, His desires become our desires. When the desires of our heart parallel the desires of the Lord's heart, joy results.

## A Heart in Relationship

God can test our heart by testing our relationships, as the life of King David illustrates. After David was first anointed king, every one of his relationships turned sour. Saul sets out to kill him (1 Sam. 18-20), and David's own soldiers later threaten to stone him (1 Sam. 30). God wanted to learn if David would remain true to Him even as his relationships with people crumbled.

God wants to know which means more to us—His approval or the approval of our fellow human beings. The apostle Paul knows that, once we seek the will of God, we will experience greater spiritual warfare and that one site of that warfare will be our relationships with people. Paul first talks about our relationship with the Father and how we are to be filled with the Holy Spirit (Eph. 5:18-21). Then he writes about relationships—with our spouse, our children, our employees, and our employers (5:22-6:9). In Ephesians 6, we are told to be ready for spiritual warfare because Satan attacks us where he knows we are vulnerable, and we are vulnerable in our relationships with people.

## A Heart of Love

In his letter to the Ephesians, Paul speaks of the mystery of Christ and the church (5:32). When I asked God to show me what this verse meant, He directed me to John 17, a prayer of Christ which reveals how the love relationship between the Father and the Son is similar to the Son's love for the church.

The great mystery concerning Jesus and the church is the incredible love that He and the Father have for one another, and this is the kind of love that Jesus wants us, His followers, to experience (John 17:26). When our value system is based upon a love for the Father, love will flow out of us. When we are bitter or hurt and love has not cleansed us, then we will not be able to love our spouse. We simply cannot give what we don't have. If a man does not receive love, he will not be able to love his wife. If a man does not know the love of God, he will not know how to love his wife.

My wife and I used to have, on average, an argument a month. The arguments increased to twice a month and then to almost once a week. My wife is a beautiful person, filled with the joy of the Lord, and I am very aware of how close I came to losing her. But she would do something, and I would feel great rage inside. The rage wasn't against her; it was against all the hurts of my past. But when she did something that reminded me of my father, I felt a powerful anger. I would put the mask of my dad on Helen's face and feel a bitter, intense rage which I directed at her.

Despite the books I read and the exercises I tried, I couldn't do enough to make this rage inside of me change. A romantic love for my wife simply wasn't there. I felt certain passions, but there wasn't that kind of selfless love a marriage needs until I asked God to show me the mystery of love that He was talking about. When I met God the Father in the wilderness and began to release my pain, I found a new love in me that could only have been put there by God. Once I experienced the love of the Father, I began to love my wife as God commanded. Helen and I may have our differences, but we have real joy in our relationship. We work together and it is wonderful.

I am also finding a joy in other relationships. I used to isolate myself. I didn't like people, and I didn't like to spend time with people. But a new joy in relationships came with my new joy in Jesus. My heart and therefore my values are changed.

## A Heart That Bears Fruit

In John 15:5-11, we are told that one of the joys of our new relationship with Jesus is to bear fruit for Him. What kind of fruit is our heart going to bear? Whatever we're doing with our life, what effect will it have five or ten years from now? What kind of fruit is it bringing to the kingdom of God?

Our occupation needs to support our ministry rather than being our reason for living. Every believer is a minister, and that perspective can bring excitement and joy to any job. We can find value through our ministry as homemakers or accountants, in sales or education—wherever we are working and ministering. We can experience the joy of bearing fruit for the kingdom, whatever our job.

## A Heart That Is Pure

When James writes in his epistle, "purify your hearts" (4:8), the Greek shows a passive verb which indicates that the purifying is done to us. We can't purify our own hearts. God has to do this, but we can put ourselves in the position to be purified by God.

❖ First, we must acknowledge our need for a purified heart. Only with a purified heart can we experience a fresh passion for Jesus. And we enable God to purify our heart by ***refocusing our expectations***. Many of the hurts we carry around in our heart have come because our expectations were unfulfilled. People have not always met our needs. They have let us down and disappointed us. As we mature, though, we can refocus our expectations and look toward God, not human beings. At times, God intends for certain of our expectations to be fulfilled through people. But if they miss it, God doesn't miss it, and in His sovereignty He will fulfill those expectations. We are dependent not on human beings but on the Lord for the fulfillment of our deepest longings. Ultimately and finally, all of our expectations are fulfilled by God.

❖ Refocusing our expectations involves ***releasing others***, especially parents, from our bitter judgments and fully ***forgiving*** all offenses against us. If we don't forgive those people who have hurt us, we ourselves will not be forgiven (Matt. 6:14-15). If someone didn't fulfill our expectations and if another person betrayed us, we are to release them from our judgment and fully forgive their actions. At the same time, we are to correct our offenses against others by asking for forgiveness and making restitution for whatever we have done.

❖ In preparing our hearts to be purified, we not only have to forgive but we have to ***receive forgiveness*** for offending others. Many of us ask for God's forgiveness for offending someone, and we need to do so. But we also need to ask for forgiveness from the very person we hurt. We need to clear up all offenses if we know that we have offended someone. (Let me add, though, that the circle of confession should only be as large as the circle of offense.)

But what if we don't know where the person lives now? What if the experience happened long ago? We need to pray for God's guidance and be ready to respond. I remember one woman from my distant past whom God brought to my heart to seek her forgiveness. I tried to reach her but couldn't find out where she lived. One day when my wife and I were standing in line in a cafeteria, guess who was right next to me! And that has happened more than once. When God convicts us of something, it is important to follow through on it and to know that He will help us do so.

Part of that following through is planning how we are going to ask forgiveness. Sometimes people who have had an affair say that going to the person they were wrongfully involved with could cause all kinds of problems. In that situation, maybe a phone call is better. Even in a phone conversation, though, use discretion. We need to let the Holy Spirit lead us. We need to ask God whom to ask forgiveness from, how to ask forgiveness, and what His timing is.

## Why Asking Forgiveness Is Important

God's command to forgive is a command given out of His love for us. Consider what happens when we ask to be forgiven by someone we've offended or hurt.

❖ Asking forgiveness is a Christian witness. Jesus said, "Blessed are the peacemakers, for they shall be called sons of God" (Matt. 5:9), and when we ask forgiveness, we are being peacemakers.

❖ Asking forgiveness keeps us from having a judgmental and condemning attitude toward others. Asking forgiveness reminds us of our own hurtful actions, thoughtless words, and blatant disobedience to God's commands. Besides, whenever we pass judgment on another, we condemn ourselves because we are guilty of the same acts and attitudes (Rom. 2:1). A judgmental attitude often comes when we are feeling guilty: we justify our own actions by judging others as being far worse than we are. Such a perspective clearly does not free us to love people.

❖ Asking forgiveness results in a clear conscience. We are then able to be transparent before God and in our relationships with others.

❖ Asking forgiveness releases us to receive the blessings of the Lord, and sometimes those blessings come through trials. God will allow people to intend something for evil, but He will turn it around for our benefit and allow us to bless them. One time a businessman made a strong commitment to a matter that concerned me, and I made a significant decision based upon it. Not long afterwards, this man violated our agreement and, because of some differences, went against his promise. I was very disillusioned and disappointed by this. Then I read a verse in 1 Peter which says that we are not to return evil for evil but we are to give a blessing instead (3:8-9). I remember telling God that I wanted to bless this person, but I knew that I first needed to forgive him.

Later that week, I saw this person at a men's prayer breakfast. As I sat there thinking how insensitive and wrong he was to violate his commitment, I realized that I had not yet forgiven him. At this breakfast, we put everyone's name in a hat and drew the name of the person we were supposed to pray for during the week. Of course you know what happened! I got his name. But that's not the end of the story.

Within the next month, he made right the wrong he had done. Great blessings came to his life as well as mine through this particular experience.

As this story exemplifies, forgiveness allows us to be released to receive the blessings of God (not only as we forgive others, but also as we gain a clear conscience). Too often, our offenses close the door on relationships God intended to use for blessings. When we don't have a clear conscience regarding our relationship with a brother or sister, we close the door to that relationship.

❖ Asking forgiveness prevents unnecessary judgment from the person we offended. Whenever we fail to have a clear conscience about a relationship, we give the other person grounds for anger and even revenge. Jesus commands, "If therefore you are presenting your offering at the altar, and there remember that your brother has something against you, leave your offering there before the altar, and go your way; first be reconciled to your brother, and then come and present your offering" (Matt. 5:23-24). Jesus also tells us to "make friends quickly with your opponent at law while you are with him on the way, in order that your opponent may not deliver you to the judge, and the judge to the officer, and you be thrown in prison" (Matt. 5:25). Actually, the foremost opponent we have is Satan, and I want to tell you that when we don't have a clear conscience, Satan will torment us greatly.

❖ Asking forgiveness is a safeguard against further wrongdoing. First, asking forgiveness reminds us of the consequences of our wrong actions. We are reminded of the human cost when we offend others, we recognize the pain our wrongdoing has caused, and we realize that we have done unto others what we would not want done to us. Also, the pain, the struggle, and the embarrassment we experience when we ask for forgiveness can be a further safeguard against repeating our sinful, hurtful ways. Not offending people will mean not having to ask for forgiveness.

❖ Unforgiveness has physical, emotional, and spiritual consequences. When the Holy Spirit convicts us of our sin, our immune system is weakened, we are burdened by guilt, and, lacking a clear conscience, we avoid God. In other words, we experience the physical, emotional, and spiritual consequences of our sinfulness—consequences which forgiveness can ease.

When we left our pastorate, our house did not sell for almost five years. Part of the reason, I'm sure, was that the five-year period was an opportunity for me to ask for forgiveness from the many, many people who were hurt by my sin. The Lord told me that if I found anyone who was hurt, I was to go to them and seek forgiveness—and this meant talking to several hundred people. And asking forgiveness never got easy. Each time I thought of another person, I was tempted by the fact that my actions were in the past and didn't really matter any more. But when God puts something on our heart, there is a reason for it. I've learned that if our heart is going to be pure before the Lord, we must have a clear conscience. My conscience would only be clear if I asked forgiveness of everyone I knew I had offended.

## A Heart Inappropriately Bonded

As Jesus purifies our heart, we experience a growing intimacy with Him, a deeper trust in Him, and a greater passion for Him and His kingdom. When our heart is not pure, we can not enjoy this kind of vital and rich relationship with our Savior. . . .

One day when I was going to the airport, the man driving told me that he was a Christian but that he had never felt the joy of the Lord. Neither did he have a sense of intimacy with Jesus. I asked him if, sometime in his life, he had been involved in inappropriate or immoral relationships. When his face turned red, I assured him that I did not want to shame him. He named about twenty different women and then some prostitutes whose names he didn't know. Most of this involvement had happened before he was a Christian, but some of it had happened after he became a Christian.

I explained to him that, through those relationships, he had given away the affections of his heart. That is why the Bible says, "Watch over your heart with all diligence" (Prov. 4:23). When we—like my driver—give away so much of our passions and affections, we don't have our whole heart to give to Jesus. My driver needed to pray the prayer of David in Psalm 86—"Teach me Thy way, O LORD . . . Unite my heart to fear Thy name" (v. 11). We can't unite our own heart. Like my driver, we need to ask God to unite our heart.

Throughout the Bible we are warned about inappropriate relationships that can divide our heart and keep us from God (see Chapter Six for a discussion of addictive relationships). In 1 Corinthians, for instance, Paul writes that those who are joined to a harlot become one with her (1 Cor. 6:15). Many different people I've talked to have learned this truth. When they have inappropriately formed a relationship with a person, they become bound to that person in their soul. There is a bonding of the spirit that is normal and right, but this kind of inappropriate bonding needs to be broken before we can have a pure heart before God.

I was a believer at the time I experienced an inappropriate bonding in my own life, and I was held by the cords of my sin (Prov. 5:22). I thought of Jeremiah being cast into a pit that had murky, miry mud at the bottom. It took thirty men to pull Jeremiah out of the chest-deep mud that was sucking him down (Jer. 38). Like Jeremiah, those of us caught in an inappropriate bond can't get out without help. When we are bonded in an inappropriate way in our soul, we feel the pull from another person. We feel scattered and unable to experience joy in the Lord. In those circumstances, we need to ask God to unite our heart and to sever those bonds that are inappropriate.

I prayed, "Lord God, I ask You in the mighty name of Jesus to forgive me of my idolatry. I ask that You would guard my heart and that it not be bonded where You have not led." I then asked the Holy Spirit to sever that inappropriate bond. I asked Him to release both the other person and me from the bond. I asked Him to unify my heart and then unite me to Him. I also asked to be bonded back to Jesus and to those people like my wife and family with whom bonds are appropriate.

## Different Types of Inappropriate Bonding

In order for our heart to be purified, all of our inappropriate ties must be broken. These ties include unresolved emotional issues or commitments as well as the following types of inappropriate bonding:

❖ Immoral relationships before and during marriage. Our sins can be forgiven and the inappropriate soul-bonding severed in the name of Jesus. God can release us from this bond in our life.

❖ Immoral ties with another person that may not have a sexual context is also inappropriate emotional dependency. Idolatry exists when anyone else is our life source instead of Jesus Christ.

❖ Enmeshed relationships in a family or extended family (see Chapter Ten). We can't have two emotional focuses at one time (Matt. 6:24). A negative emotional focus—such as a controlling parent who never allowed us to become what we wanted to become—can hold us in bondage. Even as an adult, we will be a child inside, a child controlled by a parent. Many people have never been released by their parents and, inside, are still a little boy or little girl. They still have a sense of being controlled, and this bonding needs to be broken if they are to experience the joy of the Lord.

❖ An abusive parent. Emotional, physical, or sexual abuse creates a fantasy bond that needs to be broken. Children who were abused have a difficult time breaking their denial that their parents hurt them because they have a fantasy of what they want their life to be. Abuse from parents also means enmeshment. When, for instance, a brother or sister substituted as a parent or the abuse victims raised brothers and sisters, they need to reposition themselves and break the parental bond with their siblings.

❖ Unresolved grief, anger, sorrow, or abandonment. Unresolved grief from past experiences can keep us in an emotional bond for years, especially when grief or anger is not allowed. A woman I counseled was ten years old when her father was shot by another man. Besides not being allowed to go to the funeral, Linda was made to believe that she had to be very strong. As a result, she was a very proper and in-control person. Although she later went through several tremendous traumatic experiences, she never grieved because she was never allowed to grieve. When Linda came to see me, she still had not found emotional closure to her father's death. She was finally able to ask God to release her from this unnatural bonding to emotions from the past and to free her to grieve. God answered her prayers. Linda was able to grieve the day we held a symbolic funeral service.

❖ Institutions and organizations. When an institution or organization becomes our reason for being, replacing God, we have bonded in an inappropriate way, and we should ask the Lord to sever that tie. At one church where I served, we had a symbolic wedding ceremony at the beginning of my pastorate. Now the intent was not wrong, but the result was. I was asked to take the church as my wedded wife, and the church was asked to take me as their pastor and wedded husband. This was inappropriate because we were tied to one another and not to Jesus Christ. This inappropriate bonding needed to be broken.

## A Heart Bonded to God

We must ask God to break any inappropriate bonding and to unify our heart and unite it to Him. That bond alone will give us the vital and intimate relationship with Jesus that is fundamental to our restoration. Once our heart is whole and that heart bond with God is forged, we—like David—will be able to give thanks to the Lord with all our heart (Psalm 9:1).

Let me say, though, that we don't need to wait until our heart is clean to "sanctify Christ as Lord in your hearts" (1 Pet. 3:15). We are to set Jesus apart and give Him the opportunity to cleanse and purify us, and He wants you and me to give Him even that part of our heart that isn't clean.

Jesus prays that God will "sanctify them [we who are believers] in the truth; Thy word is truth" (John 17:17). When we live according to God's truth, God can cleanse us, purify our heart, and transform us. The intimate relationship between God and human beings that was severed in the Garden is healed through Jesus Christ. Likewise, a heart that has been broken by the traumas of life is made whole by our God. And our relationship with God—fractured as it was by the hurts in our life and the lies that we believed—is restored through Jesus our Lord and Savior.

## *Your Own Story*

- *When we have a heart for God, we experience His purifying touch, His great love, and the fullness of His joy.*

  *What is the source of your greatest joy?*
  *When and where do you find joy in the Lord?*
  *How do you share that joy with others?*

- *Earlier in this chapter, I asked several rhetorical questions. Now I want to ask them more directly.*

  *Whatever you're doing with your life, what effect will that activity have five or ten years from now?*
  *What kind of fruit is your life bringing to the kingdom of God?*
  *What kind of ministry are you able to have in your occupation?*

- *Spend some time thinking about where you are in life and where God might want you to be. Ask Him to guide your path.*

- *What do you need to do to put yourself in a position where God can purify your heart?*

  *What expectations of people and even of God do you need to refocus?*
  *Whom do you need to forgive?*
  *From whom do you need to receive forgiveness?*
  *From what inappropriate bonds do you need to be freed?*

*Lay these needs before God, trusting Him to help you along the path toward a purified heart.*

CHAPTER ❦ THIRTEEN

# A Biblical Overview of Restoration

*After I resigned from the ministry, someone anonymously sent me a cassette tape. On it, a well-known pastor taught that once a church leader has sinned morally, the privilege of ministering is forever forfeited. At that point, I was overwhelmed by a sense of shame and failure, and I wasn't sure I even wanted to minister again. At the same time, though, I questioned this teaching. I might, like Jacob of old, walk with a limp, but the call of God was still on my life.*

s I wrote in the introduction, restoration involves more than stopping behavior which harms us and other people. It involves more than adjusting the externals of our life. Restoration is an inner process that involves mending past hurts and finding healthy ways to deal with the unmet needs of the past. Restoration is not just behavior modification. It is the active, continuous action of change in the inner core of our being.

The three stages of restoration are gaining insight into past, determining how that past is affecting us today, and then letting God turn our past hurts into present victory. Our God can and does use the hurts, disappointments, and traumas in our life to bring glory to Him and benefit and blessing to us (Rom 8:28).

## What Does the Bible Say?

Three different Greek words are translated *restore* in the New Testament.

❖ *Apodidomi* means to give back that which was lost or stolen (Luke 19:8 KJV).

❖ *Apokathestimi* means to restore to a former condition of financial, physical, or spiritual well-being (Luke 6:6-10).

❖ *Katartizo* means to mend, to furnish completely, to fix or complete. And this is the word used in Galatians 6:1—"If a man is caught in any trespass, you who are spiritual, restore such a one in a spirit of gentleness." Restoration involves completion where unmet needs have left us feeling incomplete. God's restoration will fill the vacuum in our souls from which we respond and react to life.

## Is Restoration Really Possible?

At the beginning of my restoration process, I wondered if restoration was even possible. I didn't have a value system or a philosophy that allowed restoration. In fact, I heard again and again in my mind that I could not be restored, especially into ministry. I have learned, however, that restoration and redemption are part of God's way of loving us, His people.

Listen to Peter's sermon: "Repent therefore and return, that your sins may be wiped away, in order that times of refreshing may come from the presence of the Lord; and that He may send Jesus, the Christ appointed for you, whom heaven must receive until the period of restoration of all things about which God spoke by the mouth of His holy prophets from ancient time" (Acts 3:19-21).

Restoration is at the heart of God; His desire for us is restoration. Jesus' ministry was and is restoration: His ministry is to restore us so that we can live according to God's original pattern and purpose. Jesus wants to bring His followers into Christlike maturity in their souls.

## Does the Bible Offer Examples of Restoration?

❖ I believe that we see a restored ministry in the life of Peter. Jesus says to Peter, "Simon, Simon, behold, Satan has demanded permission to sift you like wheat; but I have prayed for you, that your faith may not fail; and you, when once you have turned again, strengthen your brothers" (Luke 22:31-32). Jesus knew that Peter would deny knowing Him, but Jesus also saw beyond that to a time when Peter would be restored and take his place as the rock of the early church.

❖ Consider, too, the apostle John who, in his gospel, never once mentions his name. Tradition has it that John was young when he first became involved in Jesus' earthly ministry. Perhaps that is why he stayed so close to Jesus (Mark 5:37), but I believe there may have been other reasons. John may have had an unmet need for closeness and acceptance that Jesus met. Whether or not that was the case, we see an interesting side of John when he calls down fire from heaven on the Samaritans who rejected Jesus (Luke 9:54). This same John, however, became the apostle of love as his epistles illustrate. And this same John was the disciple to whom Jesus committed His mother (John 19:26-27) and the disciple with whom Jesus shared his revelation. A man apparently lacking in self-confidence and needing acceptance was made whole. With the restorative presence of Jesus in his life, John served His Lord as missionary, gospel writer, author of the three epistles on love, and recorder of "the Revelation of Jesus Christ," the last book of the Bible.

When Peter and John followed Jesus, they weren't perfect, but Jesus doesn't require us to be perfect and whole before we follow Him. In fact, Jesus says, "I came that they might have life, and might have it abundantly" (John 10:10). Jesus enables us to experience healing and wholeness when we turn to Him with our unmet needs and hurts from the past.

## Where Does Restoration Happen?

Often, we experience God's healing love and presence in His body, the church, and that is how it should be. In Galatians, the church is issued a command to that effect: "Brethren, even if a man is caught in any trespass, you who are spiritual, restore such a one in a spirit of gentleness . . . Bear one another's burdens, and thus fulfill the law of Christ" (6:1-2).

But how is the church responding to this command today? Are we too often telling a person to stop a certain behavior rather than gently but firmly coming alongside that person to help in the battle? When it comes to restoring a fallen brother or sister, do our actions tell them that they better take care of their needs and their hurts on their own? Or are we welcoming them into the church for encouragement, healing, accountability, and hope? In obedience to Scripture, we in the community of faith are to reach out and restore.

Church members can, for instance, respond to the cry for fathers I hear throughout the church. This cry reflects an important aspect of restoration: people need to release the hurt and pains of the past, much of which is grounded in their childhood. In response to this cry for fathers, believers can offer the unconditional love which heals and which many people never received from their natural father. Members of the church can also serve as spiritual fathers, an important role in the life of a person who is journeying through the restoration process and who needs to be reminded of God's truth and held accountable to His commands.

## Will People Accept Our Restoration?

Those of us who do turn to God's people in the church can learn an important lesson from the parable of the prodigal son (Luke 15:11-32). Note that when the prodigal returns from the faraway land, having spent all of his inheritance, he does not demand acceptance. Instead, he plans to ask his father to take him on as one of his hired servants. Like this son, we must be willing to ask only for mercy; we must not demand acceptance.

The good news of the gospel, though, is that God the Father lavishly pours out His grace upon us. We don't have to walk in shame, disgrace, or self-pity. We must, however, walk in humility, knowing that God will bring us forth—as the father brought forth the prodigal—when He is ready to use us. That is why the prophet says, "I will bear the indignation of the LORD because I have sinned against Him . . . He will bring me out to the light, and I will see His righteousness" (Micah 7:9). When God brings you "out to the light," you will experience His grace in abundance. He will put a robe around your shoulders, a ring on your finger, and shoes on your feet, and He will host a never-ending celebration of your restoration.

## Does God Restore People to Ministry?

❖ I heard a man on television say that only one New Testament Scripture speaks of restoration. My question for him is "How many references does it take?" I would also ask him to take the Bible in its entirety and remind him about a pattern in its teachings: If something is mentioned only a few times in the New Testament, it is amplified in the Old Testament, and vice versa. There is, for instance, limited mention of Melchizedek in the Old Testament, but there is an entire chapter about him in the New Testament book of Hebrews. Likewise—and more relevant to our topic—restoration to ministry is specifically mentioned only once in the New Testament, but the heart of almost all of the Old Testament prophets is restoration. We need to remember that the only Scripture the early church had was the Old Testament. Consequently, the members of the early church would have fully understood restoration from the writings of the prophets they knew so well.

❖ Others arguing against people being restored to ministry ask, "If a United States citizen were in prison, wouldn't he or she lose the right to vote?" They argue that we can't set a lower standard for the body of Christ and those members who sin in violation of its laws. I answer this argument with the fact that we can not establish truth on the basis of human examples. We can illustrate truth with human examples, but we can only establish truth on Scripture. Their argument is simply not valid.

❖ Another argument for not restoring someone to ministry is based on Paul's statement in 1 Corinthians 9:27—"I buffet my body and make it my slave, lest possibly, after I have preached to others, I myself should be disqualified." While Paul does speak of being disqualified, commentators point out that he is referring to the struggle against sin and that, if he fails in the struggle, he may miss out on (be disqualified from receiving) the heavenly rewards that come with serving God.

Also, it's important to note that the word *disqualify* in 1 Corinthians 9:27 is the word for *reprobate* in Romans 1:28 (KJV), and that link seems to point to the fact that some people—those who deny the very Lord who taught them His ways and shared with them His ministry—will never be qualified to minister again. Those who will never minister again are characterized by a wicked heart rather than a weak character—and this is a crucial difference. I see David as a person who had a weak character, but Saul had a wicked heart. David sought God's approval; Saul was seeking man's approval. Peter (whom we looked at above) was restored to ministry. He had a weak character, in contrast to Judas who had a wicked heart. Restoration did not take place in Judas because there was not repentance in his heart.

## How Does God Work His Restoration?

God is a God of restoration and redemption, but He works His restoration in a variety of ways.

❖ God often uses an enemy to judge the sins of His people and bring them back to His ways. The prophet Habakkuk first struggled with why God kept blessing Israel despite her sin. Then he struggled with how the Lord could use a nation even more wicked than Israel to judge her sins. Habakkuk was seeing God use an enemy as His hand of indignation.

❖ Judgment can take place within the body of Christ, but that judgment should not involve the kind of mocking and ridicule of fallen church leaders so popular today. We in the church will be judged for these actions.

Besides showing us how God judges, Scripture shows that a period of probation follows a period of judgment, and this probation may occur in the wilderness. It is in the wilderness that we are often drawn to God. In the wilderness, we can come to recognize our sinful ways and repent of our evil thoughts and actions. Of course there is not a magical number of years for this kind of probation or healing. A person can be out of ministry for two years and still not be healed. He may be out of ministry one week and be healed, but the people he has hurt may not be healed yet. That is the reason there needs to be spiritual authority. We need the guidance of the people of God as we journey towards wholeness and possibly a new ministry.

## What Have I Learned about God?

On my journey of restoration, I have learned some amazing lessons about how God restores, and Scripture bears out the truth of these lessons.

❖ *The greatest area of failure will be the greatest area of blessing.* Consider how the boisterous, impetuous Peter who once denied Christ was used by God to preach the sermon at Pentecost and open the door of faith to the Gentiles. And then there's Paul, the one who wreaked havoc among the early church and later became a builder of the very church he tried to destroy. Be encouraged, as I have, by these New Testament examples and by God's promise to restore the years that the locusts have eaten (Joel 2:25).

❖ *God restores quality as well as quantity.* It is in God's nature to give more than was lost. Solomon spoke for God when he said, "Men do not despise a thief if he steals to satisfy himself when he is hungry; but when he is found, he must repay sevenfold" (Prov. 6:30-31). Jesus offered the following instruction: "If anyone wants to sue you, and take your shirt, let him have your coat also. And whoever shall force you to go one mile, go with him two" (Matt. 5:40-41). God's justice requires more to be given than was lost or stolen, and God's grace gives more than required.

❖ *Restoration—especially the element of discipline—needs to take place under the direction of spiritual authorities* (Gal. 6:1). I submitted myself to a group of godly men who reached out to me, held me accountable to my process of restoration, and offered counsel when I asked. Their presence on this journey and their genuine concern for me have been and continue to be invaluable.

❖ *Wounded sheep cannot heal a wounded shepherd.* When a church tries to discipline its leader, it doesn't work. All discipline that I have found in the New Testament is under the direction of spiritual authority.

❖ *Nothing can distort the grace of God and keep Him from doing what He is doing in our life.* Whatever you are dealing with and however black your darkness, God is there to restore. Corrie Ten Boom once said to me—as she said to so many others—"There is no pit so deep that God is not deeper still." There is no night so dark that God will not bring the morning star; there is no night so long that dawn will not break. The mighty name of Jesus can be a source of hope for restoration, and in His time, God will use the pain of the past to bring glory to Him and blessing to you.

## Again, How Is Disbelief Related to Our Systems?

All sin patterns are rooted in the system of lies that stems from our failure to believe that God is able to meet our deepest needs and longings. The writer of Hebrews warns us about such unbelief—"Take care, brethren, lest there should be in any one of you an evil, unbelieving heart, in falling away from the living God" (3:12). And falling away is exactly what happens unless and until we face our unbelief. Only when we are convicted of our unbelief by the Holy Spirit will we be able to break free of our sinful addictions and systems of behavior and move on toward spiritual maturity.

Any sin pattern in which we are trapped is based on a system of lies. I walked where I walked because I believed a lie. If we can identify and expose the lie, then we can receive God's truth. But receiving the truth does not come through knowledge or information. The truth needs to touch our spirit and our soul if we are to experience change from our sinful ways.

The process of restoration is not a quick fix. Such an instantaneous act is not within God's plan or design for our spiritual growth. Like our physical growth, our spiritual growth happens gradually. As little children in our faith, we see the grace and mercy of God. As young people in faith, we begin to see the acts of God. When we are more mature in our faith, we will understand the ways that God works and see history from His eternal perspective (1 John 2:12-14). We don't become spiritually mature or fully restored in a day. Our growth is a process over time, but let me assure you that it is a process which God blesses and guides.

## Your Own Story

- *Write in your own words the lesson on restoration from the prodigal son.*
- *In your opinion, does God restore people to ministry? Explain why you answered as you did.*
- *What is God teaching you about Him on your journey to healing, restoration, and joy?*

CHAPTER ❦ FOURTEEN

# A Framework for Restoration

*Our daughter and son-in-law were preparing for their first child, and I was helping them get the nursery ready. I felt a little strange in paint-covered Levis—I was much more used to suits! But now that I had resigned, the days of eating out in nice restaurants and working in a plush office were gone.*

*As I sat on the floor painting the recently purchased used furniture, anger and pride rose up inside, and I began arguing with God. "This isn't what You called me to do!"*

*During my early lunch break—a brief time-out for a bologna sandwich, potato chips, and a soft drink, all neatly packaged in a paper bag—I continued the conversation. "Lord, I was called to preach!"*

*Then that still small voice spoke in my heart, the voice that I always know is from the Lord: "What you're doing is holy. . . . It is holy to serve others. . . . It is even holy to paint your daughter's furniture."*

estoration is a process, a complex and difficult process that is different for each one of us. And restoration is more than being restored to what we want to do; it is more than doing. Restoration involves becoming and being the person God wants us to be.

Before you close this book and continue on your journey of restoration, I want to share the framework which has guided my journey and the writing of this book. The promises of God as expressed in the Beatitudes Jesus shared in the Sermon on the Mount have offered hope and guidance to me. I trust that God's Word will offer the same to you.

## "The Morning Star Arises"

How well I remember the day when a well-known Christian leader called me on the telephone about two years after my resignation. As I've shared, he simply asked if he could interview me about the restoration process that I had gone through up to that point. After the interview, I recalled the Scripture that God had held up to me as a promise—"And so we have the prophetic word made more sure, to which you do well to pay attention as to a lamp shining in a dark place, until the day dawns and the morning star arises in your hearts" (2 Pet. 1:19).

This verse refers to the writing of the prophets in Scripture, but it seems to have a more personal level of meaning as well. I believe that this verse from 2 Peter calls each of us to receive the Word of God as a promise for us personally. When the Word first comes to us in the form of personal application or a promise, it may appear as only a small lamp shining in the darkness, but even a little light can dispel much darkness.

Earlier on the day of that phone interview, I had been meditating on the promise which the Lord had given me: "You will be an example of my mercy and restoration." For the first year after my resignation, I didn't have much hope in this promise being fulfilled. Everything seemed dark. I stayed home quite a bit. And I didn't hear from people who weren't sure what to say to me or how to be there for me. It was a time of isolation except for a number of Christian leaders who committed themselves to me as I started to work through this process of restoration.

Almost two years later, a man called and asked me to speak in his church. He said, "Now I know that you have a very busy schedule and are probably already booked. We are a small congregation, but we felt led of the Lord to ask you to come and speak." What he didn't know was that I had absolutely no schedule at that time; I didn't have anywhere to go and speak. When he asked me to speak, though, I wondered if he knew my story. Assuring me that he did, he said he believed that God had directed his church to ask me to come and minister to them. He also hoped his church could minister to me—and it did. When I visited that little church in the North, I witnessed a tremendous moving of God. His presence among us was strong; we knew His glory and His power during our time together.

Most of my restoration back into ministry was somewhat dark and I did not know what the future would hold. I did short-term counseling, always referring people to those who were better equipped or professionally trained. I felt more like a Good Samaritan as I encouraged people to go somewhere else to receive help. This couldn't be the restored ministry God had promised, but at times I doubted if God even wanted to work that kind of full restoration in my life. All I could do was keep walking, a day at a time.

### "Joy Comes in the Morning"

The day star is the brightest star in the eastern sky just before the dawn breaks and the sun rises. Those of us who have been in the wilderness and experienced the dark night of the soul know the importance of that day star, whatever form it takes. In the wilderness, Moses had his burning bush. In my dark night of the soul, God gave me the morning star. Both were God's indication that the long night was almost over. As David wrote in the psalms, "Weeping may last for the night, but a shout of joy comes in the morning" (30:5). On the day of the phone interview, I saw the beginnings of the fulfillment of my day star promise. That interview was God's way of encouraging me.

The dawn did not immediately break, but the hope and encouragement I had received made the darkness easier to bear. Now, as I write this book, I can tell you that not only has the day star risen, but the whole dawn has begun to break. God had promised, "You will be an example of My mercy and restoration," and I am seeing the fulfillment of His promise in this book and also in tapes, videos, seminars, and conferences. It is as though the horizon of opportunity has opened up to me throughout His kingdom.

And if the horizon of opportunity has not yet opened up to you who may be going through a wilderness experience, let me encourage you to trust in the God of all hope. Someday, in His time, your day star will rise, the dawn will break, and the joy will come.

And that "someday" may come sooner if we understand how we are responding to our wilderness experience. Remember from Chapter Two the different ways people go through the wilderness?

❖ Hermits have been wounded deeply, and they have believed lies that give them a distorted view of God, themselves, and life. Not wanting to be with people, to deal with the present, or to face the future, hermits isolate themselves in their one-person caves.

*If you have been a hermit, my prayer is that you will come out of your seclusion and into the warmth of God's love. And may God provide you with a friend you can trust, a friend who can be a caregiver and a truth-speaker as you journey toward restoration.*

❖ Nomads wander aimlessly through the wilderness, trying to find hope and purpose totally apart from what God has promised them or desires for them. Like hermits, nomads are believing lies about God which prevent them from building a life on the foundation of His truth.

*If you have been a nomad—not believing that it is still possible to lay hold of God's promises to you—my prayer is that you will find our Lord faithful. He is willing to carry you through and guide you beyond the wilderness into the promised land that is overflowing with His blessings.*

❖ Pilgrims enter the wilderness with the intention of only passing through. They are headed somewhere; they have a sense of purpose. They have failed, they have received God's correction, and they are headed for the promised land of milk and honey. Along the way, they will begin to experience God's design for them.

*If you are a pilgrim, my prayer is that you will continue to respond to God's grace and develop a Christlike character and a passion for His kingdom. And, as you experience restoration, may you, like Moses, be able to lead others through the wilderness you have traveled; may you, like Peter, strengthen the brethren; and may you, like Paul, comfort others with the comfort you yourself received.*

## "Blessed Are . . ."

Today, many programs and methods for restoration are available, but the program that will forever be true is based on the Beatitudes. These words of Jesus offer a framework for those of us who are walking the journey toward wholeness. Read closely these words of our Savior:

> "Blessed are the poor in spirit, for theirs is the kingdom of heaven.
> Blessed are those who mourn, for they shall be comforted.
> Blessed are the gentle, for they shall inherit the earth.
> Blessed are those who hunger and thirst for righteousness, for they shall be satisfied.
> Blessed are the merciful, for they shall receive mercy.
> Blessed are the pure in heart, for they shall see God.
> Blessed are the peacemakers, for they shall be called sons of God.
> Blessed are those who have been persecuted for the sake of righteousness, for theirs is the kingdom of heaven.
> Blessed are you when men cast insults at you, and persecute you, and say all kinds of evil against you falsely, on account of Me.
> Rejoice, and be glad, for your reward in heaven is great, for so they persecuted the prophets who were before you." (Matt. 5:3-12)

Notice how the nine Beatitudes can be divided into three categories which, I believe, reflect the three basic steps of restoration:

### Breaking Our Denial

We must admit our problem and our need. We may have blocked out memories from the past, but we are undoubtedly living out the pain or the emptiness of the unmet needs.

❖ "Blessed are the poor in spirit . . ."—When we are poor in spirit, we are aware that we are spiritually bankrupt. We know that we are spiritual beggars, people without any spiritual resources for the journey of life. In order to be restored, we must recognize that spiritual bankruptcy. This recognition comes when we compare ourselves with God's standards of perfection and acknowledge our shortcomings and inadequacies. We must recognize our powerlessness over our addiction and, at the same time, God's power, His love, and His ability to meet our needs.

When we admit our failures, our sins, and our addictions, we are breaking the denial that says we don't have any problems and that we are doing just fine in life. We can then turn to God and recognize His power and His provision for us through Jesus Christ. Our spiritual bankruptcy is the key to recognizing and running to the power of Jesus Christ, and Jesus Christ is the key to our restoration.

❖ "Blessed are those who mourn . . ."—Once we recognize our spiritual bankruptcy, we must experience something of the hurt caused by our sin. We must mourn the reproach we have brought upon the kingdom of God. We must understand how we have broken the heart of God by suppressing the truth about Him and His love for us. Such godly sorrow works repentance. As we grieve how our actions have hurt God and His people, we also grieve over the sins against us. This sorrow frees us from the pain we've carried and frees us to move on to healing.

I encourage people to get in and out of this phase of the restoration process as quickly as possible so that the feelings don't become self-pity. Still, we must take whatever amount of time necessary to recognize and truly mourn God's loss, the loss of others, and the loss that came into our own life because of our addictions, failures, and sin. As we cast these cares upon Jesus, the peace which He gives—the peace that passes all understanding (Phil. 4:7)—will be able to flood our hearts and our minds.

❖ "Blessed are the gentle, for they shall inherit the earth . . ."—Breaking denial doesn't come with simply releasing the past. We must also be able to look at our actions through new eyes of understanding. And that understanding comes with accepting the truth and trusting that God will work everything together for His glory and for our benefit, in His timing and in His way.

Gentleness or meekness is not weakness; it is being able to trust God. And this trust involves the godly wisdom that is discussed in

James: "The wisdom from above is first pure, then peaceable, gentle, reasonable, full of mercy and good fruits, unwavering, without hypocrisy. And the seed whose fruit is righteousness is sown in peace by those who make peace" (3:17-18). As we recognize our spiritual poverty, as we mourn over loss, and as we clothe ourselves with gentleness and trust in God, we can walk more fully into restoration.

## Refocusing Our Passion

At this point in our restoration, we sort out our values system and revise it according to God's ways. We re-anchor our souls by setting our affections on things above and developing a passion for the Lord. These next three beatitudes offer a guide for doing just that. Since our passions and values are the basis of our goals, decisions, and actions, our passions and values need to be grounded in Jesus if our life is to bring glory to Him.

❖ "Blessed are those who hunger and thirst for righteousness . . ."—It isn't a problem to hunger and thirst, but a problem can arise depending on what we hunger and thirst after. If we attach our hunger and thirst to something or someone other than God, we become involved in idolatry. If, however, we see the truth in Jesus and hunger and thirst after God, we will find ourselves satisfied by God's Word and His presence.

Scripture teaches that human beings do not live by bread alone but by every word that comes from the mouth of God (Deut. 8:3; Matt. 4:4). When we feed upon Scripture, God feeds our heart. In this communion with the Lord, our thirst is filled and, in fact, the parched and thirsty ground of our life becomes a garden from which others can taste the good fruit of Christ's love.

❖ "Blessed are the merciful . . ."—Jesus taught that it is just as important to forgive others as it is for us to be forgiven (Matt. 6:14-15). First, our forgiveness of others frees us from an attitude of bitterness and judgment and so frees us to receive God's love. Also, our forgiveness is an offering of love and mercy to our fellow human beings. But our lack of forgiveness breeds anger and hatred; it is a failure to love others and, by extension, a failure to love God. As the apostle John noted, "the one who does not love his brother whom he has seen, cannot love God whom he has not seen" (1 John 4:20). If we haven't forgiven those we can see, we can't love them and neither can we love God.

Furthermore, if we feel bitterness, anger, and hatred rather than forgiveness and mercy toward a brother or sister, we will not be able to totally refocus our passions on God and His kingdom. We will not be able to be emotionally focused solely on God. When we show mercy and forgive others, we release them from our bitter judgments and our expectations. We recover the emotional energy spent on anger and bitterness, and we can invest that in our love for God.

❖ "Blessed are the pure in heart . . ."—How pure is your heart? A look at our motives, our goals, and our purpose in life will help us answer that question. Consider from an eternal standpoint what you are pursuing in life. Does your work bless others or only you? Does it build God's kingdom or does it build your kingdom? What do you value in life? Do these things glorify God or bring status and recognition to you?

If your answers to these questions reflect a less-than-pure value system, ask God to give you a new passion for Jesus so that, like David, your heart will pant after God (Psalm 42:1). Ask Him to purify and to cleanse your heart so that, in obedience to Christ, you will "seek first His kingdom and His righteousness" (Matt. 6:33).

## Repositioning Our Relationships

We need to regain our sense of dominion (a sense of our purpose in life and the degree of control we have in life) and receive from God a pure heart. This happens when we reposition our relationship first to God and then to other people.

❖ "Blessed are the peacemakers . . ."—Most important of the relationships which need repositioning during our journey of restoration is our relationship with God the Father. Through the blood of Jesus, we can have peace with God. Then, when we remove all idolatry from our lives—when we release those systems by which we tried to meet our needs apart from God—we will have repositioned our relationship with God so that He is in the rightful position as the very source of our life.

As we make peace with God, we will also be able to make peace with people whom we have shamed and wronged, especially members of our family and those to whom we are accountable spiritually. I publicly asked forgiveness for the wrongs that I committed against the people in my church, and I also talked on the telephone with several hundred people and asked their personal forgiveness for my deception and betrayal of their trust. God directed me to be a peacemaker for a period of time, and all of us must do this. Some people will not forgive us, and others will need some time. In both cases, we will have to leave it to the Lord.

❖ "Blessed are those who have been persecuted for the sake of righteousness . . ."—Having repositioned our relationship with God as the most important relationship in our life, we will be living with His approval in mind. The approval of our fellow human beings will not be as important to us as the approval of our heavenly Father. We will even be willing to suffer persecution as we seek to please God, and, if that persecution comes, we will be able to count it all joy, knowing that God's favor is more important than the world's (James 1:2).

❖ "Blessed are you when men cast insults at you, and persecute you, and say all kinds of evil against you falsely, on account of Me."—The message of this beatitude is similar to that of the preceding: When we reposition our relationship with God, we find ourselves more concerned about receiving God's approval than the approval the world offers. We can rejoice in God even when we are spoken against because our desire and focus is His approval, not the approval of people.

❖ "Rejoice, and be glad . . ."—We will experience a new joy and peace when we are able to stand alone, strong in our restored relationship with God and our restored relationships with other people. Some people may still speak evil against us, judge our motives, and question our restoration, and we can never demand their acceptance. Instead, like the prodigal son, we can receive God's mercy and rejoice in His acceptance.

As our soul is restored to wholeness, we will then be free to lose our life for the sake of Jesus Christ and the gospel: "For if anyone seeks to save his life he will lose it. But if he will lose it for the sake of the gospel and the kingdom of God, he will find it and he will find joy unspeakable and full of glory" (Matt. 16:25).

May God bless you with strength to release your unhealthy systems of behavior, hope to keep going when the darkness seems overwhelming, and trust in His goodness as you journey towards a celebration of His gracious gifts of healing, restoration, and joy.

## Your Own Story

- *What beatitude speaks most specifically to you in your restoration process?*
- *What changes have you made in your life or your way of thinking as a result of reading this book?*
- *Look back to the introduction and your answer to the question about why you chose to read this book. What have you learned about the restoration process? What hope have you found here?*